A SCIENTIST LOOKS AT BUDDHISM

MANSEL DAVIES

BG

The Book Guild Ltd

Sussex, England.

The Book Guild Limited
25 High Street
Lewes, Sussex
First Published 1990

Set in Baskerville
Typesetting by Hawks Phototypesetters Ltd
Copthorne, West Sussex
Printed in Great Britain by
Antony Rowe Ltd
Chippenham, Wiltshire

British Library Cataloguing in Publication Data
Davies, Mansel
A Scientist Looks at Buddhism
1. Theravada Buddhism
I. Title
294.3'91

ISBN 0 86332 467 3

This writing was inscribed with his permission
— and remains dedicated to —
George C. Pimentel (1922-1989)
Professor of Chemistry,
the University of California at Berkeley:

fils de Lorraine
scientist par excellence
colleague and friend sans pareil

CONTENTS

The fundamental teachings of Gautama, as it is now being made plain to us by the study of original sources, is clear and simple and in the closest harmony with modern ideas. It is beyond all dispute the achievement of one of the most penetrating intelligences the world has ever known.

H. G. Wells
The Outline of History: Chapter XXVI 1921

"You are mistaken Professor Nietzche in thinking my ideal a purely negative one . . . I, too, have my heroes: my successor Jesus, because he told men to love their enemies; the men who discovered how to master the forces of nature and secure food with less labour; the medical men who have shown how to diminish disease; the poets, the artists and musicians who have caught glimpses of the Divine beatitude. Love and knowledge and delight in beauty are not negations: they are enough to fill the lives of the greatest men that have ever lived."

Ascribed to Gautama by Bertrand Russell.
The History of Western Philosophy 1946

The true Buddhist, however, does not need to be coerced by hopes of heaven or fears of hell: nor can he imagine a higher sanction than that of of reason.
Those who do not admit the sufficiency of reason cannot be called Buddhists.

A. K. Coomaraswamy
The Buddha and the Gospel of Buddhism 1916.

I

Introduction

One motive alone has sufficed to persuade the author to prepare this volume. So greatly have I appreciated the enlightenment which has come on reading selected works on Buddhism that I feel impelled to share some insights with those who may not be aware of them.

There is already a very large literature on Buddhism, with many (especially recent) popular accounts in English. My own interest differs from that in most such accounts: it is more specific and probably less committed. Certainly, I am only a layman in Buddhist studies and an indifferent disciple of the greatest teacher of whom I have knowledge. It is the absence of major contradictions between the ideas of science and most of what can be claimed to have been the teaching of Siddhattha Gotama that has so impressed me. This will form a recurring note in the chapters that follow.

The plan of this account is to present here, in the Introduction, a brief summary of salient features in what will be recognized as Theravada Buddhism. This will help to orient readers who are quite unfamiliar with Buddhism and, it is hoped, it will provide a background against which the fuller accounts which come later can be more meaningfully placed.

After the Introduction there follows a section sketching the status of the sources from which Theravada Buddhism draws its basic teachings, and an outline of the traditional account of Gotama's life. These are needed as a background to the core of this presentation which comes under the heading "Aspects of Buddhism". In that section there are observations on several major features of Buddhist doctrine, most of them shared by many of the numerous divisions in the Buddhist world, but all of them firmly emphasized by the Theravada school. It is of interest to consider to what extent these aspects can be directly ascribed to Gotama himself. That historical aspect is considered. However, it is much less significant than the fact that they have been taught for two thousand years as part of Gotama's teaching. Without question, they owe their status to his inspiration.

Tradition has it that Sid-dhat-tha Gotama, whose father is described as the head or lord of the clan Gotama, was born in Nepal ca. 563 B.C., and lived in northern India for eighty years. Known in history as Buddha (i.e. the enlightened one), he insisted that he was only a teacher, that he had no knowledge of, or connection with, the supernatural; that he was in no way to be worshipped, but that his teachings were to be studied and, when appreciated, followed.

He taught that everyone can achieve enlightenment, that is, an understanding of the world in all its variety and an understanding of the human predicament within it. This understanding will allow one fully to appreciate the human situation, and so to live as not to add unnecessarily to one's own or other human suffering. Each individual must come to his or her own perception of the truths taught by Gotama, and each must be aware that there is no outside source which can free one from the trials of this human condition. Self-deception is a major source of our burdens: as is the idea that life is likely to be free of distress. "Call no man happy until he is three days dead."

Buddhism is (for me, and for the followers of the Theravada school) not a religion: it has nothing to worship. Adherence to the truth is the supreme virtue. No absolute truth can be found: it can only be approached the more closely with ever greater experience. The truth is "that which prevails", and it prevails when it is not found wanting, however fully tested. Tolerence is an essential in Buddhist thought and behaviour: it is not something added on to conduce of civilized behaviour. Violence in any form, under any pretext whatsoever, is contrary to Buddhist teaching: but this does not mean that it is permanently absent from the Buddhist world. Tolerance and non-violence taken together have given Buddhism a permanently non-aggressive stance on the world's stage. Its missionary efforts lack the zeal of the religions (Judaism, Christianity,

Islam) in which faith or belief in some supreme power is all-important. Persecution is completely foreign to Buddhism.

The first images of the Budda appeared at least three centuries after his death. They were not intended for worship nor are they so treated, except in error. They serve to recall to the disciple the character of the teacher: they help to create an ambience for meditation: and they act, by their very form, as a reminder of the peace he sought to bestow.

In Buddhism, emphasis is laid on knowing and grasping, that is, clearly appreciating a number of simple propositions, not on faith or belief. "With right wisdom, he sees it as it is": this is a frequently recurring comment in the records of Gotama's teaching. A famous simile which he used (and here his brilliance as a teacher is apparent) is that in which he describes his teaching as a raft: it is a means to carry a person across dangerous waters to the safety of firm ground, where one can progress further. The teaching is not principally to satisfy intellectual curiosity or to provide a logically sound doctrine to which his disciples must subscribe. His precepts are merely the means to achieve the state of enlightenment which provides its own security and satisfaction. The raft is then no longer needed.

Already it has been suggested that Gotama was a teacher of genius, apart, that is, from the value of his teaching. What is the basis for this claim? Well, briefly, he reduced his ideas to the simplest concrete form. He lived in a non-literate world where writing was scarcely known and so he taught in such a way as to help his listeners *remember* his statements. This makes the fully written-out accounts of his discourses extremely tedious to read: they are so frequently full of repetitions. A subject will be posed in a series of slightly varying questions. The answers will come in a full sequence, matching the several questions: often there is a rhetorical repeat of the sequence to maximize retention of the message. This procedure was essentially a mnemonic device: it helped secure good definition in the mental retention of the sermons.

In addition to this particular technique, Gotama undoubtedly possessed what can only be described as a profoundly effective appeal for his listeners. Part of this derived from his own translucent clarity and his calm confidence, both characterizing the message he wished to give. There are few, if any, good teachers who are not completely conversant with and entirely happy about the content of their teaching. He insisted on his humanity. He always shared the trials of his disciples. Perhaps most important, he never spoke as though he had some god-given message. His tone was that of the enlightened teacher who understood the difficulties of others.

When doubters or opponents of his teaching challenged him, and that was not infrequently, he rarely made a direct rejection of their position. Usually he would appear to accept it, and then show what unacceptable consequences would follow from it. He was employing essentially the process of *reductio ad absurdum*, familiar in the west from Euclid's geometry. And he would illustrate his themes with stories of instances of such charm that one of the greatest pleasures in the Buddhist literature is the huge number of such attractive stories. They are an important element, not only in conveying the substance of Buddhist teaching, but also in establishing the character of its founder and his message.

Gotama emphasized that each listener must himself consider and acquire his own convictions on the correctness of what he taught. His themes were illustrated with examples from daily life. Not infrequently, they were actual occurrences, known to his audience. He rarely attempted intellectual, metaphysical, or supernatural justifications for his teachings; he reduced the essentials of his message to a small number of specific points.

What were Gotama's teachings? Comments on the sources from which they are derived will come later. They consist of those truths which Buddha considered were the minimum essential to one's understanding of the human situation and for the wise person's behaviour. The problems in life are many: from birth to old age, decay, and death, the path is rarely without its dissatisfaction, pain, grief, distress. One aim of Buddhism is to minimize these.

The Buddhist canon is summarized in the four basic truths and the eightfold path.

The four truths have somewhat the same status as the axioms of Euclidean geometry. They are:

(i) Human life is an experience beset with hazards: non-awareness of these can result in pain, grief and despair. Few, if any, completely escape such distress.

(ii) The source of suffering in the individual's life is

selfishness and restless desire, in all their manifestations.
(iii) It follows that one must aim to eliminate selfish desires, to achieve the cessation of unease, to attain the extinction of longing. Complete achievement of this aim — and here the Buddhist ideal sets a standard of perfection — means the individual has arrived in nibbana (Sanskrit: nirvana). This state of calm detachment is not to be imagined as occurring in some other world or in some other existence: it is to be aimed for in this world.
(iv) The fourth truth is the eightfold path. Gotama ennumerates the steps necessary to enhance the control and elimination of selfish desires. This, the Buddhist programme for freeing the individual from the toils of this world, is the middle path: so called because it rejects the pursuit of self-satisfaction, as also the pursuit of self-mortification. The path has eight lines which fall into three strands: Conduct: right speech; right action; right livelihood. Discipline: right mindfulness; right effort; right concentration. Intelligence: right thought; right understanding.

Of course, the Buddhist canon expounds these aspects at length. This summary merely shows how Gotama crystallized his teaching into easily remembered headings: four truths: eight paths: three virtues: and two essentials — compassion and wisdom. Little wonder that for twenty-five hundred years Siddhattha Gotama has been accepted by so many as "the great doctor for the ills of the world".

It is seen that the teaching is not a religion. It is offered entirely in a spirit of reason. Certainly, it has propositions for which incontestable proof cannot be given. This also is so for the Euclidean axioms. That the evil and pain of the human predicament arises from ignorance and selfish desires is Gotama's own thesis. He did, of course, justify, expound, and explain this fundamental tenet.

As with the major religions and world-philosophies, there are numerous schools of Buddhism, probably more than there are of Christian sects. They include the tantric form of Tibet which is a mixture of some Buddhist principles and of shamanism (primitive spirit worship): the major Mahayana school which incorporates much belief in innumerable spirits and previous incarnations, for which no evidence exists: many

Japanese schools, some of them including elements of Shintoism: Chinese schools which mix in irrational elements (e.g., from Taoism) to produce, *inter alia,* Zen Buddhism. Brief accounts of these will come later.

The present account is based entirely on the Theravada school of Buddhism which thrives principally in Sri Lanka, Burma, Thailand and Cambodia. Theravada means "the teaching of the elders", a name appropriate for an exposition derived, by almost universal agreement, from the earliest documentary records of Gotama's teaching. These are written in Gandhari and in Pali; the latter is a language perhaps as old as Sanskrit and having the same relation to Gotama as Aramaic to Jesus: i.e., if not precisely the same, it is very close to the language used by the teacher. Pali is the literary form of the Magadhi dialect native to Gotama.

The earliest texts are generally explicitly clear that Gotama would have nothing to do with the transcendental ("the other world"). He rejected the idea (and it has never been more than an idea) that there is a Supreme Being supervising the Universe and life in it. There is no everlasting soul in humans. The universe is one undivided existence: the world is a single small unity where all categories merge one into another. The man, the tree, and the mountain stand in a continuous relationship. Hence the symbolism in multi-armed, open-hand figures of Buddha representing Gotama's enlightenment, supposedly extending to all the other worlds which he already envisaged.

2
Origins

Historical sources

In the Pali sources of Theravada Buddhism there is a much quoted dictum: *Sabbadanam dhammadanam jinati* — Of all gifts, truth is the greatest. Despite this high regard for truth, no certainty can be claimed for details in the life of Gotama, nor for what can safely be accepted as being his own statements.

The reasons for such uncertainties are clear. Buddha, as he became known, lived in the period *ca.* 563 B.C.–483 B.C. This made him the contemporary of Confucius (557–479 B.C.): Lao-tse (580–510 B.C.): Pythagoras (*ca.* 560–500 B.C.): Thales (624–545 B.C.): Aeschylus (525–456 B.C.): Parmenides (539–470 B.C.): Heraclitus of Ephesus (*ca.* 530–470.; "*panta rhei*" everything flows). Thanks to his disciples and the widespread public attention in his life-time, far more detail was eventually recorded of Gotama's life than is available for any of the Greeks mentioned. However, it is impossible to establish the authenticity of the details. Knowing the period, the environment, and with other records pertaining to his life-time in Northern India, consistency and reasonable likelihood are the criteria leading to a qualified historical picture. Also, there is the undoubted fact that Gotama made a notable impact on his contemporaries. His disciples must have been interested in his life story. Whatever details were fabricated to heighten its significance, it would be difficult to deny that they must have started with some cold facts. The problem is to tease these out from the accumulated embellishments.

More relevant than his remoteness in time is the fact that his community had not acquired, to any significant degree, the art of writing. History and poetry were still transmitted verbally.

In this context, the Vedas, one of the main roots of Hindu culture by which Gotama was surrounded, stand in close analogy with the works of Homer, in that all had come down by recitation from generation to generation. Only after Gotama's day did the Upanishads come to be written.

One feature which quickly strikes a Western student of Buddhism is how small a consideration for historical veracity, or concern for valid origins, is to be found in many Eastern sources. Only the growing influence of Western scholars has led, in the last century, to any adequate appraisal of historical validity in Buddhist and other teachings. Here one must distinguish between Chinese and non-Chinese cultural attachments: no people have been more assiduously devoted to precise historical records than the Chinese. But Buddhism arose in a far different environment and, historically, it was already the subject of extensive distortions before it reached China, replete with magical elements, some five or six centuries after its founder's death.

Western concern with the historical basis for its religious beliefs is itself a recent phenomenon. It is just two centuries since Gibbon's account of early Christianity appeared. Much of Europe and most of South and Central America has not yet benefited from the insights which Gibbon and later historians have provided.

A side-light on this situation is found in *The Imperial Dictionary of Universal Biography*, a major work of scholarship published in Edinburgh and London in the 1850's: with contributions from leading scholars of its period, it runs to four and a half million words. One Henry Grove (1683–1738), "a learned dissenting divine" who, incidentally, "published An Essay towards demonstrating the Soul's Immortality", is given a succinct notice of twenty-four lines. In an entry totaling eighteen lines one learns: "Gotama, a celebrated Indian philosopher of a remote age . . . is chiefly famous as being the reputed author of the Nyaya, a well-known system of oriental logic." The writer of this note nicely demonstrates a still-persistent feature: he was unable, as indeed are many visitors to the East today, to distinguish between the Hindu and Buddhist. The Nyaya is one of the important works of Hindu teaching. The eighteen-line entry on Gotama illustrates the appalling obscurity in which most Eastern teaching remained in Europe until this century.

All the early records give detailed accounts of Gotama's peripatetic progress through towns and villages over a period of forty-five years. A large number of the locations can be identified in modern India and the pattern of his movements is itself quite convincing. More significant, of course, are the accounts of the innumerable discourses or sermons which he delivered: these become the *suttas* in the records. Inevitably, and reassuringly, many of the suttas have very similar or parallel contents. The consistency supports their authenticity.

Dependent as he was upon oral transmission of his teaching, Gotama adopted reiteration as a means of ensuring his message was retained for later re-communication by his disciples. Typically his discourses or discussions with those seeking instruction consist of a series of questions exploring the topic under discussion. In the same sequence as the questions, there may first be given a series of simple, even naive, rhetorical answers, each perhaps prefaced with "Do you think that . . .". Then the sequence will be repeated, with Gotama's considered replies. These may then be repeated with some such further preface as "And so you see that." This means that the pattern of the discourse will have been repeated perhaps four or more times, the authentic version at least twice. When translated and read today, such a sequence can be unbearably tedious. It was not intended for the printed word. It was a means of promoting the effective memorization of the teacher's message. This feature in Gotama's discourses has been reiterated as it is relevant in the context of the fact that none of them was written down for, perhaps, three centuries after his death, and the earliest copies we have of such original records come six centuries after his death.

The most complete early accounts of the Buddha's career and teaching are the Pali records. We must first follow what they claim happened.

The Pali annals include a circumstantial account of Gotama's death. This is a completely natural narrative, with elements suggestive of truthfulness, and appearing to offer little, if any, departure from likely circumstance. Following this there comes a description of what has been called the first Buddhist Council. Shortly after Gotama's death, his closest disciples gathered at Rajagrha and collaborated in groups to arrive at agreed versions of the rules for the monastic order (the Sangha), and agreed versions of the teachings (the dhamma). Nothing could be, or was, written down: all teaching was still transmitted orally for up to three centuries. Many modern scholars, having no material evidence for this first council, have doubted or dismissed its occurrence.

A second Buddhist council, held at Vaisali (*ca.* 340 B.C.) is said to have produced some documentary record of the first meeting and of the statements then agreed upon. Already separate sects were in existence. Interestingly, no-one appears to doubt this: that it should have happened is extremely plausible.

The most important single early record of Buddhism was that commissioned by the emperor Asoka himself (*ca.* 250 B.C.). Of the reign of Asoka (269–232 B.C.) in the history of Buddhism, a brief account will be given later. He ruled what was, for two thousand years, the greatest Indian kingdom. What has become known as the third Buddhist council was held at his capital city, Pataliputra (now Patna), and the leading participants are named. The differences between the sects were now substantial. Asoka had himself accepted the Buddhist teaching. Among the inscriptions which he caused to be raised, and which are still extant, it seems that he promoted the expulsion of one group. Later this grew into the largest and most widespread branch of Buddhism, the Mahayana school. Most important, presently, is the claim that at this council a definitive form of Buddhist teaching was recorded. This is now known as the *tipitaka,* the three books, often called "the three baskets". It comprises the three main canonical divisions of the Buddha's teaching: the *vinaya* (the code of discipline for the monks): the *sutta* (discourses of Gotama): the *abidhamma* (philosophical and psychological commentaries).

Many accounts of Buddhist sources suggest that the earliest Pali manuscripts, which belong to the Theravada school, could be ascribed to the first century B.C. Although the originals no longer exist, leading Western scholars affirm that about 30 B.C. monks in Sri Lanka wrote down the Pali canon for the first time in history.

In 1962 the late Professor John Brough, one of the great experts on early Indian writings, concluded that the earliest *extant* Indian text was the Gandhari birch-bark manuscript of the Dharmapada, part of the Sutta Pitaka (the book of discourses). This consists of some 350 verses of Buddhist lore. The nature of birch-bark serves to emphasize how very liable to disintegration were such early writings. Other early, perhaps contemporary, Pali and Sanskrit versions of the same text are known. These differ in the choice and arrangement of the material but "the amount of common ground is nevertheless impressive". (Brough). Gandhari and Pali are both vernacular forms of the language we know as Sanskrit, which became its established literary form.

The Sanskrit text is the longest and, probably, the latest of these three, as it shows the accretion of additional matter. The Pali version is the most coherent and has been given pre-eminence in Theravada studies. It cannot be proved to be the most authentic record of early Buddhism, except insofar as it is the least embellished. These texts show that the doctrinal basis of two different Theravada sects was remarkably uniform. It is a certain conclusion that behind these available texts there were earlier writings now not available. The Gandhari text is dated, by general impression, to the first or second centuries A.D., i.e., some six centuries after Gotama's death.

Modern studies of early Buddhism extend beyond the written sources. They refer to archaeological, iconographic and cultural aspects. These suggest that there probably were significant differences between the early recorded teachings and the practice of Buddhism. Here, one can get into a fine tangle, mostly irrelevant for my purpose, which is to assess the sources of what is now taught as Theravada Buddhism. The most important link with what Gotama taught is through the records of that teaching.

The third, Asoka, council is, significantly, called in the Mahayana School, the first council. The disagreements which came to a head there were broadly those between a conservative group claiming (how correctly is a subject for debate) to restrict themselves to the specific terms of Gotama's own teaching, and a group of disciples who accepted a broader interpretation of Gotama's mission. These latter, in a well-known syndrome, adopted the essentially realistic and supposedly historic canon to embrace substantial elements of a transcendental or magical character. These elements would certainly have had (indeed, they still have) notable popular appeal. They would markedly reduce the difference between the Buddhist and the traditional Indian — what today we would call Hindu — outlook.

It is claimed, not improbably, that Sanskrit versions of Buddhist teaching were also prepared at the Asoka Council. They eventually formed the basis of the Mahayana school. In such differences as exist between the Sanskrit and the Pali records there is, *a priori*, no reason to suppose the Sanskrit may not be of equal authenticity to the Pali. However, as I understand it, the Sanskrit versions have far and away the larger element of supernatural embellishment. Whatever other criteria might suggest, the accretion of supernatural elements can in no way point to a concern for veracity. This must contribute to the traditional view that the early Pali versions of Gotama's teaching are to be preferred.

It will be clear that nothing approaching certainty can be claimed for the priority of authenticity of these early sources. What appears to be established is this: the main features of the Theravadin Pali account — which is what I embrace under the term Buddhism — are generally common to, or are accepted by, the other schools, and are not inconsistent with the other records. Where these latter differ is principally in the appearance of large elements of the supernatural. These decorative items, stimulating though they may be to the imagination and so to artistic creativity, do not support authenticity.

Quotations from a specialist source may sharpen this assessment. In Dr Richard Gombrich's thesis (Oxford University Ph.D., 1968) he refers (p.57) to a work published in Rome in 1956: E. Frauwallner, *The Earliest Vinaya* (i.e., monastic rules) *and the Beginning of Buddhist Literature.* Of this Gombrich writes: "Frauwallner has shown that a large part of the Vinaya Pitaka, including a biography of the Buddha on which all subsequent biographies are based, was composed about 110 years after the Buddha's death, and presupposes a good deal of earlier material. The precision of his deductions, which place some Buddhist scriptures nearer the events they purport to describe than can be securely done for the Christian gospels, is unlikely soon to be improved upon." This is an interesting evaluation from an informed source but, in my opinion, it is best accepted with reserve.

Perhaps the earliest solid material evidence of the Buddha's career is found in the form of pillars erected by Asoka. One of these stands near the small town of Lumbini, thirteen miles from Nigliva, and still within Nepal, but near the Indian border. This pillar carries the inscription:

> When the king (Asoka) had been annointed (i.e. reigning) twenty years he came himself and paid reverences at this place because Buddha Sakyamuni (i.e. the wise teacher of the Sakyas) was born here. He both caused to be made a stone bearing a lion: and caused a stone pillar to be erected to show that the Blessed One was born here. He granted the village of Lumbini freedom from taxes and the payment of only an eighth part of its product.

Other inscriptions record that Asoka became a Buddhist 218 years after Gotama's death at the age of eighty. On this basis Gotama's dates are given as 563–483 B.C.

Asoka was accepting what he was told by his contemporaries. There can be little doubt that the memory of Gotama and his teaching had been carefully preserved by his disciples. To deny the existence in the sixth century B.C. of the person we learn of as Sid-dhat-tha Gotama borders on the impossible. He encountered a number of other significant historical individuals: the locations of many events in his life are established: the consequences of his life seem irrefutably substantial. Many will rightly be disturbed to find that the accounts of his life suggest it was accompanied by supernatural events. There are several, even in the Pali sources. But in northern India in the sixth century B.C. such addenda were inevitable in an account of any revered person. Even the highly rational Greeks had their interventions from Olympus. Above all these uncertainties of personal record, the over-riding consideration is that it is the teaching ascribed to Gotama which is of ultimate significance. My concern is with the content and relevance of that teaching. Conclusive in this context is the frequently recorded insistence of Gotama himself that the *dhamma* (teaching) is all.

The background to Gotama's life

The emphasis in Theravada Buddhism is on the human character of Gotama. There is no suggestion of his being a heaven-sent saviour or liberator of mankind. He is a gifted individual who became a supremely effective and beneficent teacher. His life fitted naturally into its period and into the communities of northern India where it was passed.

Northern India — in the Brahmaputra and Ganges area — was, in Gotama's time, divided into three or four major states, each having several smaller dependencies. These latter, in turn, were often divided into essentially tribal groupings. This meant there was a considerable flux in affairs, as the interests and allegiances were frequently changing. Although fighting and warfare were not unknown, they did not dominate the scene and, in any case, fighting was largely confined to the warrior caste.

The changing pattern of state allegiance was paralleled by a persistent stirring of ideas and beliefs. The almost universal background of these beliefs were the Vedic hymns embodying the praise and worship of long-regarded nature dieties (the sun: the storm: fire: rain: etc.). Controlling, in fact dictating, the constant ceremonies and worship of these deities were the Brahmins, the hereditary members of the highest caste. One of their duties was the accurate retention and transmission of the Vedic scriptures. There were clear indications from about 800 B.C., that the autocratic role of the Brahmins was being challenged, mostly by small groups or individuals. These insisted on their own interpretations of the Veda, or they propounded their world views, views which extended from the most sceptical and materialistic to the limits of magical mysticism. Amongst the more respected of these groups were the ascetics. These took themselves off to the forests or mountains, often living on the minimum of material subsistence, punishing their bodies and not infrequently, in their weakness, being plunged into trance-like states.

Nearly all these devotees of religion shared basic ideas or concerns derived from Brahminical exposition of polytheistic Hinduism. They included the concepts of *kamma* (cause-and-effect), *atman* (the soul), *yoga* (mental discipline), *samsara* (cyclical recurrence), *nibbana* (in Sanskrit, nirvana: the ultimate achievement), *samatha* (tranquility), etc. These concepts were in no way the expressions of blinkered, sectarian concern. They had the widest, in thought, universal, significance. And the present universe was envisaged as existing for a day in the eye of the Hindu creator-god: this day being equivalent to 2,160 million years. Thought was thus opened on a broader canvas than was to be achieved in the West for many centuries.

One of Gotama's predecessors in the lively Indian religious scene was the leader known to us as Mahavira (the Great Hero: 599–527 B.C.), the latest and greatest of the Jain prophets. It is important to emphasize that the Jains had long rejected the seemingly endless panoply of Hindu gods. They formed an Olympus of some twenty-four immortal saints. They despised the caste system: and they had infinite respect for life in all its forms. Gotama showed notable respect and sympathy for the Jains.

The account of Gotama's early life

The nature of the sources of Buddhist lore has already been briefly explained. More than two hundred years elapsed after Gotama's death before records were prepared. At best we have late copies of these. By the beginning of the Christian era (i.e., 500 years after his death) there were already many different flourishing schools of disciples, each with its own tendencies to emphasize, and, in many cases, inclinations to invent, details of his life for which they could not possibly have had any evidence. The Mahayana sects produced fanciful accounts, not only of the supposed previous lives of the individual who eventually became Buddha, but they also elaborated them with references to the saints *(bhodisattvas)* and spirits who had actively promoted his progress. Such fables were entirely in keeping with the preferences of Hindu beliefs.

At the same time, the accounts which carried these fabricated elements usually reproduced, as the core of his earthly life, those natural details which are the meaningful content of our earliest written Pali accounts. Even these latter contain much embroidery. It is, perhaps, especially in relation to his early years that a process of careful filtration is needed if there is to be any approach to sober fact. As soon as he achieved his enlightenment and acquired disciples, it is plausible to accept that these disciples retained clear memories of his subsequent life and his teaching over a period of forty years. This claim seems reasonable in view of the general concurrence in alternative versions of many incidents and many sermons: furthermore an entirely consistent and convincing picture of Gotama as a person emerges. Many details are compellingly spontaneous and life-like: if invented, they are inventions of genius.

The many accounts of Gotama's life — in Pali, Sanskrit, Tibetan, and Chinese — all agree on the characteristics of the man and his behaviour. In reproducing the story there is no suggestion that the details are correct, but they are details which have been incorporated into Buddhist traditions and form an engaging part of Buddhist iconography.

Stripped of obvious fabrications, the accounts of Gotama's life takes a well-defined pattern. His father Sud-dhodana Gotama was the chief of the Sakya clan, who were of the warrior caste, centred at Kapilavastu in what is now south Nepal, near the present Indian border. There Siddhat-tha was born not, it is true, of a virgin, but the birth is often described in the later accounts, as being accompanied by miraculous events. His mother died soon after his birth and he was reared by an aunt. In these circumstances, being the only child of his mother, one can accept that the father was particularly anxious for the boy's future. Not surprisingly, some accounts retail omens and even marvels portending his future eminence. Circumstantial details are offered to establish both that Siddhat-tha was unusually sensitive to tragic suffering which came to his attention and that his upbringing was so arranged as to shelter him from such events. Whilst still young he was married to Yasodhara, who, naturally, was a beautiful and devoted wife. It was more than ten years later before they had a son to whom the name Rahula, meaning "a bond", was given. In view of Gotama's subsequent emphasis on the human trials arising from personal bonds, this name, at least, is likely to be a nicely conceived imaginative detail.

Further appealing detail is offered. Now aged twenty-nine years, Sid-dhat-tha is described as enjoying riding through the town and countryside in a chariot, of whose charioteer (Channa) and horse (Kanthaka) he was particularly fond. It is much emphasized that he had been kept very carefully sheltered from the trials and tribulations of ordinary people. During a sequence of chariot excursions, he encounters, firstly, an aged man, in much distress: secondly, a sick man in agonies of pain and wallowing in the dirt: thirdly, he sees the corpse of a man recently dead. In each of these events Sid-dhat-tha establishes that he is encountering the common experience of his fellow men and women. Finally, a wandering man, with a shaven head and wearing a yellow robe, is encountered: he had abandoned the struggle of advancing his career, but was relaxed and serene in a calm acceptance of this world and its painful trials. This demeanour, despite its weaknesses, greatly impressed the prince.

This is, of course, a poetic account of a young man grasping the almost inevitably painful and tragic side of life. The incidents, although not impossible, may well have been assembled as an anticipation of Sid-dhat-tha's eventual concern with *dukkha,* the dissatisfaction which is part of human life. And they provide cause for his consideration of his goal in life, and of what contribution might he make to the reduction of *dukkha.* Of greatest relevance is what is accepted by all Buddhists: that, at age twenty-nine, he left his wife, child, his father and their home; he chose to go in search of teachers or gurus who might satisfy his desire to understand the human condition.

The original narration tells of the prince leaving his home at dead of night without disturbing the mother and child, whom he knew would provide a barrier to his intentions, but to whom, it is related, he felt he would return after his obligatory search. Taking Channa, Kanthaka and the chariot, he leaves Kapilavastu, and travels through the night. He exchanges his clothes for a simple robe. With the prince's clothes and ornaments, Channa returns to his home and Sid-dhat-tha commences his years of searching.

Years of wandering

From this point the narrative is based on Gotama's oft repeated account of his wanderings. It is relevant to sample these experiences as, even if they are accorded only a small basis in actuality, they have an important part in delineating the image of the future Buddha which his disciples accepted. In one account of his renunciation, Gotama is said to have realized that "all things hasten to decay: only the truth abideth for ever". Certainly he spoke of his wanderings as his search for truth and, irrespective of the content we find him ascribing to the truth, it always remained a never-failing preoccupation of Gotama's.

He adopted the role of an ascetic; of such the countryside had many examples. He had shaved his head and took to begging his food. Moving south of his home, to the district where there were reputedly many religious teachers, he came to the capital of the Magadha kingdom at Rajagaha (modern Rajgir). Reports of his distinguished bearing having reached the king, Bimbisara by name, the latter sent for him and engaged him in discussion.

The king reasoned persuasively with Gotama: he should use his gifts and accept the responsibility of leadership and of guiding his people. Bimbisara would welcome him as a partner in his kingdom. Power and wealth are not to be despised, and, joined with a religious committment, could lead to great satisfaction.

Gotama greatly appreciated the worthy aims the king avowed and also his generous interest. But the pursuit of the true understanding of humanity's lot was an all-consuming task. He had abandoned his ties and his prospects to that end. Better than ruling over others was sovereignty over oneself. Would a blind man with some prospect of gaining his sight abandon that prospect?

Gotama asked for no pity or even sympathy on the difficult, painful path he had chosen. Rather he pitied those who were burdened with the cares of royalty and the problems of riches. What might appear to others as great assets often produced only lasting anxieties. Quite soon the king, dead, would be coequal with a dead beggar. He was determined to find, before the chance was lost, what enlightnment the many sages and ascetics could provide. He did not wish to be entangled on this path: but he did understand Bimbisara's good intentions. He departed, promising to return when he had found satisfaction.

Inconsistencies in early records on the timing of the Bimbisara meeting suggest this account could be non-historic.

Gotama now sought out recognized religious teachers. Like the Greek philosophers of a somewhat later date, these men pursued their own evaluation of the world and human behaviour. They sat and thought, and, with a mixture of reason and mystical intuition arrived at philosophical schemes which they taught to the disciples who attended them. Two such teachers whom Gotama describes visiting are otherwise known in the Brahminical accounts of this period. The first was, by name, Alara Kalama: the second, Uddaka Ramaputta. To each he explained he had abandoned a life of comfort as it promised him no lasting satisfaction. With each he spent a substantial time: his total wanderings occupied six years. From his own account of his discussions it is clear that Gotama learned much from these teachers on the various categories in Brahminical metaphysics. They served to sharpen his critical facilities. Alara, it seems, acclaimed him as an equal. They also taught him the aims and practices of meditation. These are still a very important part of Buddhism, as also of many other, largely Hindu-derived, schools.

Although he was impressed by these teachers, Gotama was far from satisfied, He could not accept their views on transmigration nor their views on immortal individual souls. In this same period he visited many temples. With the teaching and activities in them he was very unhappy.

As he saw it, the life of man was subject to the law of cause and effect. He could find no support for the common belief that each was possessed of an immutable, everlasting soul. With clear reference to Brahminical practices, he claimed that only ignorance could persuade men to prepare countless festivals to worship doubtful deities or to arrange huge assemblies for ceremonial animal sacrifices. It would be far preferable to revere such truth as could be found than to appease the gods by shedding blood. What love can a man possess who believes that the destruction of life will atone for evil deeds?

It was near Uruvela, not far from Benares, that Gotama spent most of his six years of searching. By his account, it was a lovely wooded countryside with small rivers and many villages. As a location it could well have been attractive (his references to it show a keen sensitivity to the beauty of the natural world), but the life he chose was not. He was associated with a group of ascetics who convinced themselves, like many others since, that mortification of the flesh was the means to spiritual enlightnement. Once seriously undertaken by a person of Gotama's obvious commitment, such a life was not soon abandoned. As in the west, these hermits not only withdrew from the world but they also appeared detached in time. It could be that some element of competition arose in the severity of their practices.

It is well known that lack of minimal nourishment leads to abnormal mental states: visions, feelings of detachment, giddiness and impressions of moving through the air are frequent symptoms. These could well persuade the ascetic that he is attaining super-normal trance-like states. Gotama not only confessed, he later insisted, that he had driven himself to the point of starvation.

It is a measure of his fundamental sense of reason that, although previously convinced that this was a path to be explored (it was very much the "in" thing), Gotama realized he was achieving no valid insights by such extreme austerities. He had been joined by a group of five other ascetics and they were more than disturbed when he announced his decision to abandon self-punishment: as he left them, they derided him.

Gotama slowly recovered his strength. It was a period of recuperation from what had been, physically, a long period of ill-health. It led to the occasion, undoubtedly the best known occurrence in his life, in which he claimed to have grasped the essential truth that he had been seeking. He achieved his enlightenment.

Gotama achieves enlightenment

Although the elements of this occasion are not so remarkable, few Buddhist accounts can avoid embellishing it with some abnormal and, most frequently, supernatural quality. It is one of the few places in his story where Gotama himself seems to have invoked super-normal perception.

He had come to Buddha Gaya in the Gaya district of Bihar, and there sat himself down in a quiet spot under a fig tree of a type known ever since as the bodhi, or bo-tree *(Ficus religiosa)*. There he remained, undoubtedly in a state of well-being after his recent self-inflicted torments. Probably helped by the clarity of mind which frequently accompanies a return to health, Gotama emerged after many hours contemplation convinced that he had "seen what there is to see". He was sure that he had acquired the insight which he so much desired. It is from this time that he can be called Buddha: his insight was neither born with him, nor was it god-given.

It may be helpful at this point to indicate that the historicity of this occurrence is on as good a basis as anything we know of Gotama's contemporary Pythagoras, the accounts of whom have been described as explaining *obscurum per obscurius*.

Of course, the accounts of Gotama's "awakening" in most Buddhist literature are replete with impossible and unnecessary fantastic detail. Some Mahayana versions would require little less than a new geological epoch to have arisen.

So central to the whole of Gotama's career as a teacher was this traumatic experience of enlightenment, which led to his acquiring the title of Buddha, that it is not surprising that his own account of it is embellished with supra-normal elements. He claimed to have seen his own progress through numerous previous existences, an experience not unnaturally stimulated by the conviction he must already have shared with the whole community in which he had lived that re-incarnation was an universal experience. And the occasion is dramatized in later accounts by his reported unsuccessful temptation by Mara, the lord of the world of passion.

The relevance of such claims is not only that they were certainly acceptable to his contemporaries, but nothing less would have been expected for such a momentous occasion in the life of a potential world-teacher.

Realism returns with Gotama spending some weeks thinking out the implications of his intuitive perception of his life's message. This period corresponds to the frequently encountered interval when a scientist, having grasped a new insight, not infrequently in a sudden flash, requires some weeks to work it out and to present it in a coherent statement. Hadamard, Einstein, Kekulé, W. L. Bragg are amongst those who have recounted this experience. Furthermore, some have emphasized how the problem had been in their minds for months, if not years, with no progress towards its solution. Few in the field of scientific research would not agree that one of the major gifts is to be able adequately to formulate the question whose often long delayed answer will clarify the problem.

Gotama had spent years asking the questions which seemed to him all-important in the understanding of the human situation. He had made a determined effort to tackle the world problem, as he saw it, from many different directions. Given his determination, his sincerity of purpose, and his unpreparedness to accept a solution which did not survive his own critical appraisal, one can understand why he was eventually carried away by the enlightenment which his mind proffered.

Gotama had spent much effort with Alara Kalama, Uddaka Ramapatta and other teachers mastering the philosophy and metaphysics of the Brahmins. In these weeks of private contemplation, he gave himself the task of delineating his own philosophical as well as moral outlook. Having done so, now seated, the story goes, under a banyan tree,* he thought he would first go tell it to Alara and Uddaka. These, however, had both died. Gotama then realized that his message, with its insistence on the ephemeral nature of most of life's common pleasures, was not likely to appeal to many. His fully defined path would be too difficult for more than a few. And he hesitated. Was it a practical proposition to attempt to teach the analysis he had achieved with so much effort, "the cure for the ills of the world" which, with all realism, he could see would prove initially unattractive to most people — was it practical to teach this openly?

"I have attained this truth which is difficult to comprehend, difficult to grasp, needing much wisdom to accept. Those surrounded by darkness, immersed in ignorance, carried away by passions will not be able to see this truth which runs against the current, is deep, subtle, and hard to understand." Such, he claimed, were his thoughts.

Then comes a beautiful simile. Gotama thinks of the world as a lake: in the lake, lotuses grow: many are fully immersed below the surface: others have emerged to varying degrees: some are resting proudly on the water, having amply mastered their environment. So it is in the world. Some will achieve the full enlightenment of the lessons Gotama would teach: others would, initially, grasp only some part: many would gain nothing. With this limited prospect in mind, the Tathagata, as he preferred to be called ("he who has arrived (at the truth)"), decided he must share his insight with the world.

---

*The bo-tree and the banyan are both fig trees. The latter is *Ficus bengalensis*, the former *Ficus religiosa*. The bo-tree is remarkable for its size and longevity: the banyan is even larger, in that its branches send our aerial roots which reach the soil and form additional trunks. So extensive can such a single linked growth become that it may shelter more than a thousand persons.

This figure of speech accounts for the deep symbolism of the lotus in Buddhist iconography. Furthermore, it immediately calls to mind the similar evaluation of his public arrived at by one of the great Protestant teachers: John Calvin. The two beneficently conceived philosophies, Buddhism and Calvinism, could scarcely be further apart in their orientations, but both share the view that perhaps "only a few are chosen". Buddhism, realistically accepting that only some will be prepared to struggle free from the toils of the world, is however, far less commited to, and in no way dependent upon this element of elitism.

The first sermon

Gotama decided he would first give his message to the five ascetics who had joined him near Uruvela. When he found them, they did not welcome him. They could immediately see that he had recovered his physical well-being and, in contrast with their persistence in self-denial, Gotama had certainly indulged in food and drink. Looked at in terms of its essentials, this encounter carries conviction. The ascetics had felt disappointment when Gotama left them. Now they felt cheated by his obvious well-being. Nevertheless, his manner and his equanimity in the face of their scorn soon suppressed their challenge.

Such is the account of the background to the Buddha's first sermon. Only Gotama's own description is in the record for these initial events of his ministry. But the sermon he delivered has a place in Buddhism comparable in significance to the Sermon on the Mount in Christianity. A truly committed Buddhist would not, of course, offer any such specific comment. As will become clear, the good Buddhist would not wish to compare the path which he follows with the offering of any other teacher. We shall find that Gotama himself assiduously avoided drawing disciples from others: he frequently asked them, if they were satisfied, to remain loyal to their already chosen teacher. The elitism in Buddhism, in so far as it exists, is an elitism restricted to the seekers. They are the disciples whom the Tathagata would wish to meet.

An outline of this sermon — known in Buddhist circles, from its Pali title as "Setting in motion the wheel of truth", is important as, at least traditionally, it summarizes what Gotama initially felt was the essence of his enlightenment. Much in the whole teaching of Buddhism has its origin here. No attempt will be made to elucidate the content. The consideration and illustration of this material, in its various aspects, forms a major part of this book.

The Pali account opens with the phrase: Thus have I heard. This precedes very many records of the discourses which are amongst the earliest available. It clearly aims to suggest the oral transmission of what follows. It offers a direct report, mostly in the third person, of Gotama's message.

Addressing the five ascetics Gotama starts: These two extremes should be avoided by those who have abandoned a life of routine to search for the truth. What are these two extremes? The first is the pursuit of pleasure and self-satisfaction. This is a low, mean, unworthy, and common weakness, leading nowhere but to self-delusion. The second extreme is self-mortification: self-punishment, abstinence for the sake of abstinence, self-deprivation which cannot produce a balanced mind, but rather distress, dangerous weakness and no profit.

The Tathagata, who has experience of these extremes, has found the middle path: it leads to calmness, understanding, a sense of fulfilment, deep satisfaction, and, eventually, to nibbana. And what is this middle path? It is a path with eight strands. The individual must accept to follow the right evaluation: right thought: right speech: right action: right livelihood: right effort: right mindfulness: right concentration. This is the path that leads to knowledge, to insight, to tranquility of mind, to ultimate lasting freedom, to nibbana.

There are four noble truths. The first truth governing man's life is that of *dukkha:* from birth, one's life is a succession of trials, disappointments, dissatisfaction, suffering and sorrow: this is what one experiences. Age, grief, pain, loss, separation, and death come to everyone. Not to face this is to be blind to the human situation.

The second truth is that of the origin of *dukkha*. The dissatisfaction, suffering and sorrow are a consequence of the craving for more pleasure, the pursuit of ever new wishes, the restlessness for further enjoyment, the cultivation of greedy passions.

The third truth is that *dukkha* can be eliminated: it is possible to achieve the cessation of *dukkha*. And the fourth truth, leading to the cessation of *dukka,* is the noble truth of the eightfold path.

Such was the understanding, insight, knowledge, wisdom, enlightenment which arose in Gotama. He explained that there were three aspects to each truth: the knowledge of the truth: the acceptance of action to conform to the truth: the fact that such action was possible and had been taken by Gotama.

"When my grasp of these truths and these aspects was unclear I could not claim to have succeeded in my struggle for enlightenment. With them, I have acquired the insight which is all-adequate in this world, and which will lead me to nibbana".

The transcript from the Pali sources is a very much extended, truly long-winded, statement. One can say that Gotama, certainly on this occasion, repeated each significant item three times. This must reflect the effort which he required and which the monks were habituated to give, in learning and conveying his sermons. Such mnemonic devices were much cultivated in a world which could not write. They were expected and even promoted by commendations such as that in one of Asoka's pillar inscriptions: "Certain phrases have been repeated again and again because of the sweetness of the truth they carry and in the hope that people may act upon them."

With this sermon the Tathagata embarked upon forty-five years of travel and teaching through north-east India.

3
The Teaching of Gotama

An eclectic account: the Theravada school

When we come to consider the content of Gotama's teaching there are a number of qualifications I should like to make.

Firstly, there is the question of the sources one is prepared to accept or to use, The total canonical literature of Buddhism is immense: i.e. the sources accumulated, not to say manufactured, by the many different schools to form their accepted primary documents are equivalent to hundreds of volumes — and that apart from commentaries which have since been incorporated into their various teachings. Large proportions of this enormous bulk are devoted to the rules of the orders (monks and nuns), and the programme of activities, appropriate to the temples and in the community. More relevant for the lay student are the accounts purporting to be Buddha's teaching, and the description of events, usually encounters with leaders, or priests, or workers, in the course of his travels. It is clear that, in historical terms, a large part of these volumes is fabrication.

There are two reasons for this conclusion: one historical, the other based on content. Already a century and a half after Gotama's death a significant group of disciples argued that the simple account, of a predominantly factual character, was an inadequate presentation of the wondrous and, as it seemed to them, miraculous life and achievements of Gotama. They drifted apart from the elders (i.e. from the Theravada school). Eventually, from the council called by Asoka *ca.* 250 B.C., they separated to form the Mahayana (i.e. the greater vehicle). They do not, as I understand it, reject what the Theravadins cling to, but they insist it is only part of the message and that

Buddhism includes very much more. This they emphasized by speaking of the Theravadins (the school of the elders) as the Hinayana (the lesser vehicle).

The Mahayana school of Buddhism is its largest and, almost certainly, its most widely noted sector. In addition to huge slices of the supernatural, it incorporates accounts of many bodhisattvas, that is, imaginary enlightened teachers, symbols of a supra-mundane character serving as representatives of various ideals. The only concern I can have for these features is the question — why were they thought necessary?

Probably they carried an emotional appeal, like the archangels nearer home. At best they can be regarded as specific symbols of virtues to be attained and of achievements to be copied. It is an obvious feature of mental behaviour that the symbols and fancies of one's early years can retain a significance long after they cease to have any reality. Father Christmas is the best-known example. The Mahayana Buddhist does not necessarily claim a factual basis for his bodhisattvas: they can remind him of aspects of behaviour thought admirable in his school.

Gotama often expressed concern because his message was likely to be too deep in its simplicity. Brahminical Hinduism had conditioned most Indians to regard a multitude of spirits and miracles as the very hallmarks of religion. In this sense, the Mahayana school became a religion, in that it abandoned the limitations imposed by reason. It showed a persistent strain of Hinduism in that it readily incorporated features which were popular, or likely to appeal also in other countries, when it spread from India. Those happy to wallow in a sea of miracles, can have an enjoyable time in Mahayana Buddhism. But they need scarcely go so far in search of the factually absurd: there is an ample supply nearer home.

In fact, miraculous elements do also appear in the Pali canon and are often accepted as "natural" by lay members of Theravada communities. But it is to be emphasized that such elements are in no way essential, rather, it can be argued, they contradict the core of Theravada teaching.

These comments will make it abundantly clear that I am concerned only with a selected aspect of Buddhist teaching: that is, the teaching of the Theravada school. As a separate, well-defined school, the Theravadins can probably best be dated from the Asoka council (*ca.* 250 B.C.). One of its earliest, as well as strongest and most literate schools, has been that in Sri Lanka (Ceylon).

Buddhism arrived in Sri Lanka thanks to an historic mission. Asoka sent his son, Mahinda, with six companions to the island (*ca.* 235 B.C.). Coming with the recommendations of the most powerful emperor India had seen, the success of this Buddhist mission could perhaps have been anticipated. They soon persuaded King Tissa, his court, and the community leaders, of the virtues in Gotama's teaching. Their acceptance of Buddhism appears to have been entirely genuine. The version they were taught was that approved at the third council and it was this that was written down *in extenso* in Pali. This established the Theravada school in Sri Lanka and, despite wide fluctuations in its strength and its purity, the island has remained a focus for this early teaching up to the present. The school benefited greatly from the work of a notable fifth century A.D. scholar known as Buddhaghosa. He clarified and systematized the teaching, giving it, without departing from the earlier sources, greater coherence than had previously been achieved.

It is to the Theravada account of Buddhism that I have clung. Even a small acquaintance with the literature of this specific form shows substantial variations. One of the most important expositions of Buddhism in English came with the work of Edward J. Thomas *(The Life of Buddha: 1927)*. Despite his high standards of scholarship, it is clear, in reading his works, that he imparts, at times, a gloss of western thought in his account of the teaching. Later specialists are agreed on this and probably most European writers have a similar tendency. (The fact that the present writer is subject to the same bias will be obvious). It is important, in my judgement, to give greatest significance to those who are most fully capable of evaluating the earliest reliable sources, i.e. the Pali canon.

Fortunately, there are at least two extended, comparatively recent accounts by leading Pali scholars of Theravada Buddhist origins. The first is in a volume edited by Kenneth W. Morgan, *The Path of the Buddha, N.Y. 1956*, in Chapter 2: *The Fundamental Principles of Theravada Buddhism*, by U. Thit-tila: lecturer in Buddhist philosophy at Rangoon University and chosen by Morgan after much consultation with Buddhist scholars in Asia. The second is by Walpola Rahula, *What the Buddha Taught, Bedford, Eng., 1959, 1967, 1972:* this Sri Lankan author spent many years at the Sorbonne with one of the acknowledged European leaders in Buddhist studies, Paul Demiéville.*

I have not, I hope, departed significantly from what these two writers have expounded with constant reference to the earlier Pali sources. Where departures have been, and will later be made, they are on the sceptical side, and they especially include some features which I cannot myself accept, sometimes as lacking validity, sometimes as lacking clear meaning. Even so, what remains is more than amply valuable.

A note on the Pali language. It had been in common usage in north-east India where Gotama is said to have spoken one of its dialects. It is closely related to Sanskrit, which can perhaps be described as a polished, literary form of Pali. The greatest proportion of early Indian writings, including the Vedas and the Upanishads, are in Sanskrit which, from Sir William Jones's time in Bengal (1783–94), has been accepted as one form of the root for so many of the western, in fact, Indo-European languages. Great volumes of early Buddhist literature (especially the Mahayana) are also in Sanskrit and, not surprisingly, as Sanskrit was so much studied by western scholars, it is from those sources that the first serious expositions of Buddhism appeared in Europe. One minor consequence is that there are both Pali and Sanskrit versions for very many terms and proper names appearing in Buddhist literature, the Sanskrit forms usually being far the better known. Merely to establish that the present account is essentially derived from the Pali-Theravada canon, the Pali forms are used in it. On occasions, when it may help, the Sanskrit equivalents will also be given.

Thus we have:

Pali	*Sanskrit*
Siddahattha Gotama	Siddhartta Gautama
dukkha	duhkha
kamma	karma
nibbana	nirvana
Theravada	Sthaviravada

* Since this account was written, there has appeared: Richard Gombrich, Theravada Buddhism, London 1988.

The principal Pali canon consists of "three baskets" or three collections of teaching, the tipitaka (Skr. Tripitaka). The first is devoted to the rules and organization of orders of monks and nuns: the second consists of the sermons, sayings and the many reported discussions of Gotama with his followers and contemporaries: the third gives an exposition of cosmology and metaphysics, much of it claimed to derive directly from the Tathagata. The second of these 'baskets' is itself a very large work, divided into many sections, and available in the English translation of the Pali Text Society of London. Readily available works (Conze: Rahula: Thomas: *et al.*) quote the original sources in their record for the basic account of Gotama's teaching. The aim here is merely to summarize some of its major aspects.

The first great truth

Gotama's original exposition of his teaching, made soon after his own enlightenment to the ascetics, previously his companions, is already carefully systematized. Its structure is in the form of "four noble truths".

The first of these is the dukkha-thesis. Dukkha is a term whose translation has led to much discussion: dissatisfaction, restless inadequacy, unhappiness, pain, longing, frustration, craving, suffering — these are some translations which have been offered for the feeling of anxious *discontent* which is *dukkha*. Gotama's first truth is that *dukkha* is normally a constant accompaniment of human experience. Very simply, individuals do not achieve a permanent state of satisfaction. Whatever his/her status, successes, comforts or pleasures, the individual will, before long, reach a state of wanting something more, or something different, and becomes restless until this further requirement is approached or achieved

This proposition needs little exposition. Usually, only the very young or the very old are entirely happy with their condition: and that happiness does not last for long. There is no need to overstate the case. Some individuals can be generally quite content for long periods, but what they are likely to feel more acutely than their contentment is, at times, an aching sense of lacking some additional means to their further satisfaction. And, of course, no human life is free from mental pain and suffering. Illness and death come to the highest and lowest, and can be the source of great distress.

If Buddhism were a religion it would be necessary to insist on the acceptance of this dukkha-thesis. It surely has a wide validity but, as the Buddha constantly emphasized, there are no absolutes and it must suffice to insist that dukkha — the generally painful experience of human existence — is a principal concern in Buddhist teaching, whose aim is to eliminate or, at least, to minimize it.

Coming as "the first truth", the dukkha-thesis has, not surprisingly, been used to characterize Buddhism as a pessimistic philosophy. If a concern with the dissatisfaction or distress which individuals constantly encounter in their lives is a pessimistic stance, then Buddhism is in that position. However, — and it is probably a matter of temperament or, more specifically, of one's glandular balance — most adults would accept that life is a trial, beset with many painful personal experiences, and, in that sense, Buddhism is merely realistic.

Despite its insistence that life is not, and cannot be, a joy-ride, there is no adequate reason for writing down Buddhism as a depressing philosophy. Everyone must decide for his or herself whether life is free from disappointments, and dissatisfactions which, not infrequently, reach a pitch of grievous discontent (dukkha). The Tathagata's appeal is likely to be limited to those who do not find life a joy-ride. It is no part of Buddhist teaching that people should be persuaded of their dissatisfactions or afflictions. There is an over-riding insistence that each of us must make our own judgements, come to our own conclusions, accept our own solutions, and stand on our own feet. In this aspect it becomes abundantly clear that Gotama offered only a teaching or philosophy: no provision is made of an external saviour or dogma whose acceptance will soothe all difficulties: the emphasis is on seeking and accepting the truth of the situation: enlightenment is what the Buddha offers. A Buddhist can suggest that the acceptance of dukkha as an element of the human situation is a necessary pre-condition for any cure of its ills.

At this point it can be reasonable to suggest, that one notes the dukkha-thesis and proceeds to see what Gotama makes of it.

The second great truth

The "second noble truth" is that of the origin of dukkha. Dukkha (discontent) arises from desire, longing, thirst, yearning, craving, lust, hankering: i.e. from any unrequited wish which leads the individual to be dissatisfied (dukkha). It might be thought that the desires might be divided into categories, some more acceptable than others: thus the desire to know and to learn the truth, to do good to one's neighbour, etc. might instantly be claimed as acceptable. However, the Buddhist canon qualifies even such beneficent wishes. If they lead to an uncontrolled attachment or a craving which disturbs the individual's equanimity, then they must be restrained and brought under control. This, at least, seems to follow from the Buddha's specific mention of one thirst which can give rise to dukkha: that is, the thirst to reach nibbana. As this is the ultimate goal for the individual in Buddhism, we see that no wish or enthusiasm must become excessive.

Walpola Rahula writes (p.30): "Here the term "thirst" includes not only desire for, and attachment to, sense-pleasures, wealth and power, but also desire for, and attachment to, ideas and ideals, views, opinions, theories, conceptions and beliefs." It might well seem that this all-inclusive dismissal of all attachments must lead to an entirely negative attitude to life's interests. But, even if this is to admit an inconsistency (which the Buddhist scholar would not accept), this is not so in practice. Each of us should cultivate our interests and pleasures within a well defined moral code (see later — the eightfold path), but these must not come to dominate the individual's behaviour to an uncontrollable degree. Here the Tathagata's consistent choice of the middle path is evident. "Nothing in excess".

There is a clear, unavoidable, connection between much which is implied by dukkha and the thirst which can give rise to it. Many forms of suffering or grievous discontent can be associated with a desire which is its immediate cause: but there are also many common instances of dukkha for which the link is at most nominal and artificial. The victims of a typhoid epidemic, or starving children in Ethiopia or elsewhere, cannot sensibly be described as suffering because of a desire for good health or a desire for food. These public forms of dukkha are an inevitable part of life as normally experienced. The only "desire" which can legitimately be related to them is the desire to continue living and without that, individual existence would not endure.

Thus the forms of dukkha (grievous discontent) which are meaningfully related to one's desires are one's personal longings and sufferings: those for which the individual carries responsibility, as they arise from his/her intentions, wishes, or cravings. It is for these dissatisfactions or longings that the Tathagata can immediately offer a remedy. Expressed in this way there is an emphasis here on the strictly personal aspects of one's life.

Gotama had undoubtedly thought out the situation very thoroughly. He addresses himself to the individual and, as in most religions and philosophies (but not in political philosophies such as Marxism), he emphasizes that it is the individual who first has to be put right.

Returning to the second truth: the personal aspects of the individual's grievous discontent are rooted in his/her self-centred wishes — self gratification, self-advancement, self-interest. Selfish attitudes and selfish behaviour, claims Buddha, are the principal source of most of our troubles.* The qualifications in this sentence are important. It is the first, but not the sole cause of dukkha which is ascribed to self-centredness. Other undesirable or evil influences can be the source of dukkha. We have already indicated the typhoid bacillus and famine conditions as immediate agents.

Toynbee may well have had this Buddhist proposition in mind when he wrote: "Our man-made evils have been caused by the greed and aggressivenesss that spring from self-centredness." That puts the second truth in a nutshell.

A major element in Buddhist thought needs to be brought out at this point. An extended analysis of causality is presented in Gotama's teachings. In its simplest essence he uses the term kamma (Skt. karma), not in the sense of fate (which often tends to be its meaning in a Hindu context), but in the sense of an intentional good or evil action which will necessarily have repercussions later in the individual's life.

It is all-important to realize that a cause and effect chain is an essential feature of Buddhist thought. In a manner

*It is accepted that these are inherent in the human situation.

reminiscent of (but, historically, preceding) the Greek philosophers, Gotama elaborates a whole quasi-logical pattern in the cause-and-effect chain. The pattern is known (in translation) as conditioned development or genesis, and as the pattern is a closed cycle, it forms one basis for the symbolism of the wheel* in Buddhism. The directly relevant claim is that the deed carries its own consequences which will inevitably react on the doer. Although the linkage from the event or the deed to its results is given the status of inevitability, this is in no way to be regarded as a reward or punishment syndrome. The Buddhist view appears to be that this deterministic aspect in the world's affairs does not have its origin in moral or ethical significance, although the consequences of events can certainly be harmful or otherwise.

This neutralism in terms of ethical judgement, represents an extraordinarily mature aspect of Gotama's thought. It is of a piece with his invariable, calm detachment. Without attempting to question its correctness it must be accepted as part of the Buddhist canon: and, whatever else may be said of it, it is certainly at a very far remove from primitive naturalistic, anthropocentric ideas. Students of Buddhism will realize that a very large body of moral and philosophical writings deal with the brief comments in this paragraph.

The relation of dukkha to selfish personal interests involves the widest possible consequences. Walpola Rahula makes this clear: (p.30): "According to the Buddha's analysis, all the troubles and strife in the world, from little personal quarrels in families to great wars between nations and countries, arise out of this selfish thirst." From this point of view, all economic, political and social problems are rooted in this selfish "thirst".

It is not unreasonable to accept that a huge fraction of all the disputes in public, and even international, affairs arise from the parties being dominated by their own immediate interests. They fear losing their rights or privileges to those they identify as their opponents. In such confrontations and struggles for power, self-interest is usually only too obviously a major motive.

But some qualification may be necessary. To insist that all

*Another important origin of this symbolism is "the wheel of truth" invoked in the title of the Tathagata's first sermon: and in the circle of birth-death-rebirth — i.e. the cycle of existence and continuity.

our discontents arise from selfish motives is to elevate a generally sound principle into a dogma. Some individuals or parties in a dispute may be almost devoid of selfish motives and their sufferings may justifiably be ascribed to the selfish advantage taken of them by their antagonists. This would move the selfishness to another party without, perhaps, formally negating the second truth.

Added to, and in many cases independently of, the selfish motive, there can be simple ignorance or lack of understanding of the situation. Instances must arise when such ignorance is determinative: and, in particular, ingnorance of what might well be the better interest of one party. Such departures from the direct applicability of the second truth would not be inconsistent with another constantly re-iterated view of the Tathagata: ignorance is the greatest source of weakness.

It need scarcely be insisted that each one of us acts from day to day on the clear assumption that we are always able to judge what is best for ourselves as individuals. No-one is normally prepared to admit that our view of what is good for us in strictly personal matters is mistaken. Of course, we do go to the doctor in case of illness, and, when the condition is sufficiently acute, most people readily take his advice. But even here, the exceptions may outnumber those who conform to the course advised. The consequences of excessive smoking, alcohol, and other drugs, are too well established to need comment. And yet huge numbers are constantly being ruined by such means. These cases are the clearest instances of self-indulgence and, if not of ignorance, then of a sad determination to remain unenlightened. Medical professionals often claim that more than fifty per cent of the cases they encounter in urban areas are ones of essentially self-inflicted illness.

There can be no doubt that a calm self-analysis in the light of the Tathagata's teachings could greatly reduce personal suffering.

The third great truth

The third "noble truth" is, very simply, an affirmation that freedom from dukkha (grievous discontent) is attainable, here, in this life. The recipe for this release is simple and obvious in Gotama's view. It amounts to eliminating the desires for self-advancement or self-indulgence which the second "noble truth" gives as the origin of dukkha.

The elevation of this logical sequel to the second truth to its independent equal status lies in the "here, in this life" aspect of its claim.

We have not, as yet, mentioned the major element in Buddhist thought which accepts, unquestioningly as it seems to me, the belief that on the death of an individual a transfer takes place of some aspect of that individual's personality, or life-experience, to another new-born individual. This idea raises a host of questions on which extended comment is made later. It will suffice here to say that I can find no significant justification for this assumption, nor any worthwhile suggestion in the idea. "Personality" has been used here as an approximation to the Buddhist concept: it is of the greatest importance that no immortality of a soul or of the self is meant. The new individual can (it is claimed), in some circumstances, recall experiences in previous existences. What is relevant in relation to the third truth, is that in all these recurring existences, dukkha is present.

Gotama claimed that his teaching would so completely release the individual from dukkha as to lead to the cessation of the cycle of birth-death-rebirth. In giving no credence to this cycle, I am making a major departure from the Buddhist canon. The elimination of this speculative transcendental feature means an instant cut-off from extended areas of Buddhist philosophy: but, I would claim, the value of the Tathagata's teaching is scarcely diminished. We are merely removing an entirely unsubstantiated, unreal chapter from a book, most of which still retains its great insights and values.

The cycle of birth-death-rebirth is in no way peculiar to Buddhism. It has the widest possible circulation, from primitive peoples to advanced cultures. Gotama was immersed in communities, especially the Brahminical-Hindu, whose whole outlook was anchored to this idea. This must largely account for his ready acceptance of so ill-supported a thesis. Such accounts of Buddhist and other eastern teachings as I have read offer no reasons for accepting the idea of re-birth. The emotional attachment to the only form of being that we know has, through the ages, convinced most people that it must continue in some form. In India five centuries B.C. there was no need to offer evidence for this assumption.

There were other reasons for accepting it. As the realist he certainly was in most respects, Gotama saw that most individuals were not going to attain the degree of enlightenment and the conquest of this world's temptations which he had achieved. Remember, he hesitated whether he should attempt to teach it. The cycle of re-birth provided a means by which, having progressed only part of the way to enlightenment in one life, the individual would be able to continue his upward struggle in a new incarnation. In this way, perhaps, the Tathagata was able to envisage all eventually achieving enlightenment. It is noteworthy that whilst Gotama was amply clear-sighted completely to reject the concept of "the soul", he nevertheless accepted this weaker, perhaps somewhat less unreasonable version of life-extension. For the student of Buddhism who accepts that few will approach closely to nibbana in this life, but that most will depart finally in various unenlightened states, there is no need to be further concerned with the artificiality of the concept of re-birth.

Returning to the third truth: the claim that it is possible to eliminate all aspects of dukkha can be, and generally is, differently expressed: nibbana (Skt. nirvana) can be attained.

The concept of nibbana is one of the most widely known of Indian concepts. It ante-dates Buddhism. In Western discussions it has often, quite mistakenly, been equated to "heaven". Whilst all, even the greatest Buddhist scholars, insist that to define nibbana in words is almost impossible, its only similarity to the Judaeo-Christian-Moslem "heaven", is that it is an ultimate goal, beyond which no progress is conceivable.

The third truth is essentially a statement that the incompleteness, longing, impermanence, which are aspects of dukkha and which characterise an individual's life, are not *necessary* conditions. Dukkha can be avoided, eliminated, left behind. When fully achieved, freedom from dukkha means that nibbana has been attained. One can, therefore, accept that the aim of Gotama's teaching is to attain nibbana: adding the proviso that (in my view) nibbana in no way involves belief in a cycle of rebirths.

This aspect of Buddhism — the elimination of dissatisfaction or craving which is rooted in self-interest — is one to which a Westerner sees limitations. Is not dissatisfaction the irritation which leads people to seek improvements in their own or the community's circumstances? This can scarcely be questioned. And here we strike a fundamental aspect of the Tathagata's teaching. He was principally concerned with the inner life of the individual. Although insisting on benevolence, charity, and all good works, Gotama gave little, if any, attention to material affairs. We shall return to this omission in some later comments on Buddhism and science. Suffice it to suggest here that raising the elimination of personal dissatisfaction to a dominant aim, leads to an isolation of the individual from his environment. Detachment becomes of supreme concern. Not, be it noted, that detachment leads to satisfaction: that would almost be a stigma to a Buddhist.

It seems fair to comment that a Buddhist monk — that is, one committed above all else to attaining nibbana — is unlikely to be fired with the need, the ideas, or the effort, e.g. to improve the operation of cooking so that alternative fuels to the cow-dung of India should become available. The priest would rightly ask: "To what end?" I can only suggest that I would probably not be in a position even to think of the incomparable Gotama if the material circumstances of life had not changed radically from those in these islands in 600 B.C.

The fourth great truth

One feature of the Tathagata's genius as a teacher was his reduction of essentials to the simplest possible systematic form. Another obvious instance of this procedure is found in the Mosaic ten commandments. The bases of Buddhist teaching — one might say the rules of it — come as "the four noble truths". These present a logical sequence of tenets, which help by imposing a pattern, itself a notable *aide-memoire*.

Of all aspects of Buddhist teaching, that which is both unquestionably Gotama's own and, at the same time, the best known, is what is described in the fourth noble truth; that is, the path which gives vision and knowledge, which leads to calm, insight, enlightenment, nibbana. This is the eight-fold path.

Gotama singled out eight aspects of the individual's behaviour and comportment, each of which must be controlled and correctly directed by anyone seeking to attain the masterly composure, allied with a profound understanding and sympathy for the human situation, which he himself achieved.

There is an enormous literature expounding the eight facets emphasized by Gotama. They clearly represent an attempt, which is largely successful, to crystallize a whole programme for virtuous, moral behaviour into a simple pattern. It can help to group the eight under three headings:

conduct: right Speech: right Action: right Livelihood.
discipline: right Mindfulness: right Effort: right Concentration.
intelligence: right Thought: right Understanding.

The use of "right" in the sense of correct, morally good or desirable, receives extended illustration in the Tathagata's teaching and in Buddhist texts. Only some brief, and doubtless obvious comments are offered here.

Right speech is, like the other practices, characterized by truth, honesty, and consideration for others. It implies an avoidance of lying and misrepresentation: an absence of tale-carrying or other harsh talk which could lead to ill-will or hatred between individuals or groups: abstention from abusive or malicious language and from foolish gossip which could create unhappiness. The good Buddhist would choose to remain silent rather than indulge in harmful talk.

Such a standard of responsible speech is clearly not achieved without conscious practice. it is, of course, far more readily attained if one is brought up in a family or community already striving to achieve such behaviour. This aspect applies to all eight elements in the Buddhist path. That was one reason for setting up the *sangha,* that is, the order of monks. But the lay-person also should aim for the same conduct. The credit will be the greater if it is achieved in unfavourable circumstances.

It will be obvious in this, as in the further activities to be mentioned, that the standard set bears no relation to what is commonly accepted in the Western world. It does not follow that the Buddhist ideal is "other-wordly". What is implied is that the standard of our public communications, in speech and print, is abysmally low. In view of what is daily purveyed in the popular press and high-rating television programmes, one can ask whether any standard is now even considered? Mention of the almost farcical rulings of the Press Council and the degree of veracity in television adverts suggests it would be difficult to define a level below which the public media do not go. The ultimate defence of these, and of so many other, deplorable offerings is "they are what the public wants". The usual criterion by which this conclusion is established is that the offering should produce a larger profit, or a larger popularity, leading to the self-glorification of the agents concerned. The selfish element in such motivation is obvious.

Many readers may already be anticipating that an adherence to Buddhist standards will remove all spontaneous pleasure and enjoyment from life. Even in Gotama's own entourage this was not so. And it is not so in Buddhist communities today. But life there is, certainly, a more sober affair with a complete absence of a mindless razzmatazz.*

Right action covers major aspects of behaviour. First is respect for life in all its forms. The Buddhist is called on to avoid, not only the killing of other creatures, and especially one's fellow-humans, but also not to harm them unnecessarily. This injunction is spelt out in the strongest terms. It embraces the non-human world, because in Buddhism no ultimate distinctions or barriers can be drawn within the unity of the world.

Here, again, the profound understanding of the Tathagata can be seen. It has taken until the latter half of the twentieth century for an environment lobby to gain strength in the West. Most of its aims are enshrined in Buddhist teaching.

My understanding of the "thou shall not kill" in Buddhism is that whilst the command has the highest priority, the principle of "no absolutes" applies. There are circumstances in which a Buddhist does take life. He is not necessarily constrained, as are the Jains, from swatting midges: which the Jains protect to the extent of wearing a fine muslin over their faces when there is the chance that a midge might get into one's throat and be slaughtered there.

Controversy, it seems, has arisen on whether a Buddhist is necessarily a vegetarian. The answer seems to be: preferably, yes. If meat has already been killed without one being responsible for it, then a Buddhist may eat it. Here, as elsewhere, the line seems to be defined by whether one has any responsibility for the killing: that must not be proposed,

*How many notice that even a supposedly sober medium, the B.B.C., feels it necessary to introduce its news bulletins, which it regards as serious fare, with flashing lights, oscillating clocks, or other mentally disturbing, distracting irrelevancies?

encouraged, or actively supported. A compromise has clearly been accepted. Maybe it was fostered by the practice of the monks begging their food from the laity: if the latter had prepared meat without the monk's connivance, he could eat it. This somewhat dubious position may be paralleled by those of us who are meat-eaters because he have never been in an operating slaughterhouse. It is certain that Buddhists who regularly eat meat are compromising on their adherence to the canon.

Right action demands the responsible use of one's body, its senses and functions. Control of sexual interests and activities is a major concern: monks are celibate, the men and women lodged in entirely separate locations. There is no equating of sex with sin, as the concept of sin does not, indeed, cannot exist in Buddhism. In the sense of being deplored, of being damaging, and of leading to disruption, the equivalent of "sin" is to behave in a way which debases oneself, one's family, and one's community. Accordingly, sexual control in a lay person means avoidance of artificial stimulation, avoidance of promiscuous behaviour, and indulgence in sex only when it is based on trust, attachment, and respect.

As for the sexual appetite, so for the others. Bodily pleasures, comforts, and satisfactions are not barred, but they must not be developed so as to lead to indulgence in sense pleasures. On many occasions, it is recorded that Gotama enjoyed a particular meal: but deliberate stimulation or a pre-occupation with the pleasures of eating is not countenanced. The rule is: in all things avoid excess. Gotama's experience as an ascetic convinced him of the dangers and even delusions in excessive self-denial. The emphasis in the Buddhist rules, as I see them, is to ensure that the individual is constantly aware of what he is doing, and that his rational mind should not lose control of his behaviour.

Consistently with this principle, alcohol and other stimulating drugs are totally excluded. It could be difficult to justify this on rational grounds. Perhaps the practical view is that even the smallest amount of alcohol leads to some relaxation in one's responses: this can, and does frequently, lead to a sequence of steps towards uncontrollable drunkenness. No smallest degree of irresponsibility is to be encouraged.

Each one of us has a duty to ensure that one's life is as free as possible from suffering or hardship. This demands moderation in all things. Enjoyment is in no way ruled out: abuse of one's senses or of another person's senses is. The Buddhist world should be fully sober, but by no means lacking in enjoyment, nor without an ample range of entertaining pleasures.

Right livelihood, as with the other headings, merely summarizes a whole spectrum of concern. Any activities which would tend to make Buddhist ideals more difficult of attainment are to be excluded. Slaughtering: butchering: soldiering: arms manufacture or trading in weapons: alcohol or non-medical drug trading: these activities are obviously prohibited. Each person is asked to consider the consequences of the successful pursuit of his means of livelihood. A gun-maker would have difficulty even in imagining his product would not lead to disturbance and death: members of the advertising and news-media fraternities would be hard put to it establishing their concern for the truth: but they are in no way ruled out *a priori*.

It is obvious that a Buddhist state would have an enormously different outlook from that dominant in the Western world. Given the all-too-clear direction in which the latter is moving, the contrast is alarming. And not only because it highlights the desperate state of the so-called advanced nations. In addition to the condition of our civilization, what is being illumined is the revolution in aims and in behaviour needed to reverse our Gadarene progress.

I recall that Bertrand Russell was apt to ask his visitors in the 1960's what chance they gave of our escaping a nuclear holocaust before the end of the century. He probably rated it below fifty per cent. His constant trouble was to be some twenty years ahead of his time. As long as the star-wars scenario attracts an astronomical U.S. budget, and with other catastrophes threatened, there is no large room for optimism.

Mindfulness is a feature given great significance in the Tathagata's teaching. Awareness of all aspects of one's activities is its meaning. It represents the insistence in Buddhism that one must accept responsibility for one's path through the world. One cannot accept the views and guidance of some other person or of some established institution: nor, having subscribed to such a programme, can one happily renounce further day-to-day consideration of life's problems.

On the Buddhist path there are no sleeping travellers.

It is traditional to specify four features of the awareness that is intended.

Mindfulness of the body and its activities. This calls for a constant, unstrained, unself-conscious awareness of how the body is performing in breathing, walking, relaxing, striving, etc. This emphasis is undoubtedly related to the advantages claimed for yoga and meditative practices which start from a conscious awareness of the body-mind's normal resting state.

Mindfulness of feelings is the sense(s) equivalent of mindfulness of the body. It precludes day-dreaming. Not, it seems, that one should constantly make an effort to register what the body or the senses are doing. Rather that one should not allow them to be distanced from one's control. The aim is to become aware of how our feelings change in response to events in our surroundings. In this (and the other aspects of mindfulness) what the Tathagata is anxious for us to realize, is that the "self", which is the totality of our conscious being, is a constantly changing entity: from one moment to the next, our bodies, feelings, minds and thoughts are in flux. It is *awareness* of the arising and decay of the pattern in our total consciousness that we are asked to cultivate.

The two further parts of mindfulness relate to our mental states and the thoughts and ideas which we experience. We are asked to notice the flux in these: how one's mood changes for no too clear reason, how conscious one can become of the variety of ideas flowing in and out of one's mind. Quite clearly, all these practices advanced for our preferment, derive from the age-long development of meditation, already well cultivated in Gotama's time. This tradition does not belong to the West, but in recent years far more attention has been given it, and yoga (which is, by origin, the Brahminical practice of meditation) now has many new practitioners.

Buddhist "mindfulness" is equivalent to the promotion of a rational conscience. There is the implication that one of the highest achievements is a calm, stable, benevolent mind. Any hindrance to its attainment — such as an intention to selfish action — will be avoided by one committed to the path of the Tathagata. The end is represented in innumerable figures of the Buddha — "the peace that passeth all understanding". That is the unequivocal and easily appreciated end of the path.

Right effort is the development of a positive attitude to progress in the path of Buddhism. A constant commitment and strengthening of the will to follow the teaching and precepts of Gotama is implied. Placing this — right effort — as one of the eight paths amounts to an insistence that one must not allow oneself to do other than advance in one's understanding and use of the teaching.

A more mundane aspect of right effort is the need to be honest in one's work. The individual is responsible for applying himself so as to complete his task efficiently and well, whether it is immediately on behalf of himself or of another. In this respect "right effort" means honesty of action.

Right concentration refers maybe principally, to the practice of meditation in the Buddhist context. The various stages which the properly oriented and repeatedly exercised individual experiences in attaining the much sought state of pure equanimity are the result of right concentration. It is important to emphasize that in Buddhism this experience of a state of ultimate detachment and peace carries no element of mysticism or other-worldliness. It is regarded as one of the ultimate benefits to be gained from right mindfulness and right effort.

The exercise of contemplation, in which one calmly considers the situation one is experiencing, is also greatly favoured. The good Buddhist would regard this as necessary and beneficial, in somewhat the same way as a Christian regards prayer. The results can be similar: a detachment from one's immediate problems and a tranquil mind.

Right thought describes two main features — a condition of mind, and the character of one's intentions or motives: each of them relevant to the aims of the Buddha. In the first place, one's mind should be free from hindrance to clear thought: not disturbed by trivial considerations: "as calm and clear as a deep pool on a windless day". The thought-motives, of course, should be those appropriate to progress along the Tathagata's path: a detachment from any form of selfish interest: an acceptance of the unity of the world: a realization of the demands imposed by non-violence: and so on.

Finally, *right understanding* is the clear appreciation, a full grasping, of the Tathagata's teaching. It means having arrived at a willing conviction of the truths which he taught. With such an understanding the Buddhist acquires what is for him a completely adequate insight into the character of human existence. It might be described as the wisdom of the Buddha.

This completes a summary of the content of the eight-fold path, and, also, of the "four noble truths". The whole of Buddhism is based on these concepts, which occupy a status equivalent to the totality of the ten commandments and the Sermon on the Mount in Christianity.

The whole of this Buddhist teaching is aimed at enlightening the individual on the nature of our human predicament, and then guiding him/her in a way which will lead to a strongly reinforced calm acceptance and clear understanding of our condition. In the canon, of course, the detachment from the problems of this world takes the Buddhist eventually to nibbana. In that case, he/she no longer suffers any rebirth and disappears from this world. It is not clear how anyone becomes aware of this, except, presumably, by the great enlightenment achieved by such a person in attaining nibbana.

4
Aspects of Buddhism

Substantial experience in the laboratory teaches one that it can be unrewarding to rely on accounts of methods or processes until one has experienced them oneself. Every cook is familiar with this fact. As I have never lived in a Buddhist community nor done more than read about, and think of, those aspects of Buddhism which have attracted me, my views cannot be those of the committed practising Buddhist. Nevertheless, it seems reasonable for me to comment on those features which I regard as most significant. In doing this, I hope I shall not ascribe to the Tathagata anything he would find objectionable: certain, it is, that I shall omit much that he, and especially large numbers of his disciples, would regard as essential. In Gotama's enlightenment there is a great deal which is immediately accessible and of the greatest significance, and which is entirely open to reason.

Truth

For any scientist a major appeal in Buddhism is its concern for the truth. This is a basic feature in two senses. This concern was frequently stated by Gotama as a major aim of his teaching: and concern for the truth pervades the whole philosophy of Theravada Buddhism.

Repeatedly in the Theravada canon is the Tathagata's claim: "I will teach you the truth and the path leading to the truth". The very name Tathagata does, it seems mean "one who has arrived (at the truth)". Already we have seen that in much of his discussion, Gotama undoubtedly equated arriving at the truth with attaining nibbana. This identification might well suggest doubts as to what he meant by the truth. But there is little practical uncertainty.

Defining the truth is, of course, a metaphysical problem. Briefly, most scientists would identify it as that information which, after the most extensive testing, is supported by all the available evidence. This is no absolute criterion. We must accept that new observations may modify our views: but there can be reasonable confidence that only small differences will arise over the area in which the truth has been acceptably established for some substantial period.

A classical example is Newton's law of gravitation. Perhaps no result in science was ever more extensively or more adequately or more accurately tested. In the whole of the solar system only one extremely small deviation stood out persistently. It was one of the singular triumphs of Einstein's general theory of relativity that it was able to account for this deviation — the motion of the perihelion of the planet Mercury. This did not in any meaningful sense negate Newton's law: the only sense in which it could have done so would have been if Newton's law were regarded as an absolute truth. No practising scientist would have claimed that.

Gotama, as far as I know, did not define the truth — except by implication. He positively claimed it would set you free. Illusion, delusion, and error disappear when one achieves the truth: that was certainly Gotama's thesis. He illustrated this on many occasions by reducing false propositions to the status of delusion. It was in this sense of "freedom" that Gotama equated the truth with nibbana. And this was the whole aim, end and goal of his life's teaching.

It is in a specific but clear sense that truth and freedom are equated. Knowing the truth means one can be entirely confident in what one does in using it. Doubt disappears. To the extent that the truth is established, uncertainties vanish.

Consistent with this appreciation and pursuit of the truth was the Tathagata's insistence on the empirical approach.

Remembering that he was convinced of the supreme significance of his message, it shows extraordinary restraint and a profound confidence in '*magna est veritas et praevalebit*' — great is truth and it will prevail. This is the ultimate stance of the experimental scientist.

It must not be imagined that I suggest that Gotama advocated an empirical approach in what might be scientific studies. There seems to be little evidence that he was at all concerned himself with the analysis of natural events other than in a philosophical way. Experimental study scarcely raised its head even in the classical European world, certainly not until many centuries after Gotama. He was applying the empirical method — try it and see — to what he regarded as far more important than the consideration of nature. He was advancing it for each person to come to an understanding of the human situation, and to decide how best to cope with it.

The empirical method accepts that experience will dictate workable solutions to problems. It implies that the truth is not known and cannot be known *a priori,* but has to be found by trial. How extraordinarily different from the attitudes common to the classical and medieval European worlds! How different even from the mistaken dogmatism to be seen publicly in so many directions in the 1990's. Our classical philosophers had their extended systems which they arrived at by merely sitting and thinking (in Aristotle's Lyceum of the peripatetics, walking and thinking). As a typical result, Aristotle knew that women had fewer teeth than men. He had not bothered to count.

Some economics and much political theory has the same non-empirical approach: and with equally bizarre results. The reader will be able to provide his/her own examples.

Of course, the cosmology described in Theravada Buddhism and which were probably accepted by Gotama, is, to us, a fantastic picture. There is no need to pursue its generally imaginative pattern. It belongs to the sixth century B.C. and its details are irrelevant.

It does have, however, one remarkably significant feature. Like the Brahminical teachers who both preceded and succeeded him, Gotama spoke in the most explicit terms of other worlds and other universes than ours. By today, everyone accepts the reality of the enormous extent of the observable cosmos: but in the Judaeo-Christian-Moslem schools this observation requires departure from the original source books and the teaching of many centuries. Only incurable blindness now allows anyone to imagine that this minute world of ours was created specially for *homo-sapiens.*

The Buddhist has not only no difficulty in accepting, he has a confident expectation, of the existence of other worlds. This relates to many aspects. Gotama at no stage projected himself as some entirely unique revealer of the truth. He was happy to accept that there had been other buddhas and that more would be seen in the future. His disciples were so confident of the existence of other similar worlds to ours that reference to the Tathagata's insight being adequate for them is frequently found in their writings. In Kyoto there is a visual demonstration of this extension to other worlds. The Sanjusangendo temple (13th century) has nearly a thousand images of the Buddha, each with several outstretched arms and hands. Each open hand (a truly meaningful Buddhist image) symbolises the willingness and the ability of the Tathagata to minister to the ills of another world.

In the Theravada teaching an interesting differentiation relating to "truth" appears to be long established. This is the difference between conventional truth (*sammuti-sacca*) and ultimate truth (*paramattha-sacca*), in so far as it can be established. So many of us make such statements as "I have never known such rain": more correctly, what we wish to say is: "I cannot immediately recall such heavy rain (in June: in this country: after a spell of fine weather: etc.)". "On a clear night one can always see the stars of the Plough" (in the northern hemisphere). "Water cannot be hotter than boiling" (but what pressure is one assuming to define the boiling point of the liquid?). More significantly, we constantly use terms we probably could not define.

Such statements are "relative truth". Philosophers and logicians are constantly aware and are often rightly reminding us of the limited (if any) significance of such statements. When one is, or can quickly become, aware of their limitations, such mis-statements do not usually lead to serious consequences. Most people do not take them for more than they are meant to convey.

What is relevant is that the Theravada school has long been aware of the limitations of many common usages, and has taught this difference between conventional and ultimate truth. This generates a heightened awareness of the value of critical analysis before accepting what may well appear as a very plausible thesis.

No absolutes

Walpola Rahula makes a categorical statement (loc.cit.p.39): "According to Buddhism, the Absolute Truth is that there is nothing absolute in the world, that everything is relative, conditioned and impermanent, and that there is no unchanging, everlasting, absolute substance like Self, Soul or *Atman* within or without."

A verbal change is needed for consistency. The term "Absolute Truth" above needs to be replaced by a *non-absolute* expression such as "the attainable truth" or "the whole available truth". With that modification, the statement is one of the most significant one-sentence summaries of human experience.

As a layman in such matters, it is a precarious task for me to comment on some major aspects of Western philosophy. Nevertheless, one does know that a truly extraordinary influence on Western thought is enshrined in the works ascribed to Plato. If not the first, he was certainly the foremost to envisage, and he was sufficiently persuasive to convince generations of philosophers and theologians, of the "reality" of supra-mundane ideas which have an universal validity. Plato insists that our everyday experience of general attributes such as goodness, justice, beauty, and (even more alarmingly), our appreciation of simple objects such as an orange, a horse, or a bed, depends upon the existence of an ideal "form" of these mental experiences. Outside this world, the ideal Goodness, Justice, Beauty, Orange, Horse and Bed exist. These ideals have an absolute character quite independently of specific, knowable examples. They are eternal and absolute.

Anyone who finds this proposition ludicrous is casting grave aspersions on countless European students of philosophy over a period of two thousand years. Nevertheless, the aspersion has been repeatedly cast, perhaps most effectively by those who have introduced new concepts such as tobacco, margarine, cinema, ukulele, etc.: words each used to label conveniently a range of objects, all under one term having some common features without necessarily being identical. Few are happy to suggest that with the appearance of the first telephone some new eternal ideal Telephone had been added to the supra-mundane world: or that it had existed there from the infinite past.

Much of Plato's metaphysics derives from Parmenides (539–470 B.C.), one of the Greek philosophers who was a contemporary of Gotama's. He, like Plato, was devoted to describing "the truth beyond appearances". Both claimed one should be able to reach the absolute truth, not by an observational, experimental way, but by a process of critical, logical thought. It is Plato who is principally responsible for conveying to Europe's philosophers this concern with "absolute truth" and its extraordinary mistaken approach to knowledge. We shall see how much more meaningful and defensible was Gotama's insight.

In denying the absolute and insisting on the relativity of all our knowledge of things, Buddhism shows an extraordinary depth of insight when it is remembered that this thesis was advanced two and a half millenia ago. It can have arisen only thanks to the Tathagata's profound intuitive discernment. It is of a piece with his empirical approach.

We recall that he left his home with an overwhelming desire to find a true understanding of the human experience. Very many here set themselves such a task. Gotama did not stay in his castle, or found an academy. He took himself into the world and subjected himself to encounters, discussions, discipleship, and the experience of everyday life with a wide variety of people. In this way he must have accumulated a whole spectrum both of observations and interpretations of the human world. Again, many thoughtful individuals have done just that — but very few of our professional philosophers. If one can suggest clues to Gotama's success in his search, one must be his possession of a marvellously calm, rational, critical mind. Unprepared to indulge in fanciful ideas of a supramundane character, he remained almost entirely within the range of his own experience. Perhaps the flux of philosophies in his environment guided him away from the *a priori*. His whole approach was essentially empirical.

Whilst remaining anchored to the basic tenets of the Tathagata's teaching (that is, to the four noble truths), the empirical attitude pervades Buddhism. At no time is the enquirer told "but you must accept this": or, "we know that that is so". The constantly reiterated suggestion — coming also from the Tathagata — is, "come and see".

There are two major consequences. It is clear that

Buddhism, in the Theravada school, is not a religion. And the open-mindedness means that the Buddhist has never been embarrassed by, or in opposition to, new revelations achieved in human experience.

Science, in all its aspects, is committed to a "try it and see" approach. It is based on controlled observation or experiment. Much of the effort is directed to finding where currently held accounts are inadequate. Such findings lead to modification or extension of the previously accepted models. No scientist is tied to a dogmatic acceptance of any proposal that can be further tested. It is this, essentially common attitude, which eliminates confrontation between Buddhism and science.

In addition to this basic agreement, there are, however, specific instances where the Tathagata's insight provides a close parallel to the scientific appreciation. Mention of these will come later. Here, we return to the Buddhist denial of absolutes.

The working scientist, and more particularly the experimentalist, is constantly aware and readily accepts that our results and deductions are essentially provisional. There is no particular virtue in this provisional character, but it is forced upon the scientist who knows from experience that he (or one of his colleagues) may go into the laboratory for a few weeks and disprove what has earlier seemed a quite satisfactory account of his studies. Few, if any, scientists get sleepless nights over this uncertainty. Why? Well, because most scientific models have usually been very thoroughly tested, and the degree of uncertainty in particular circumstances has been repeatedly observed to be very low. A standard operation in science is to test the model in some new, often extreme circumstances. It is then that the interest in an experiment can reach a high level. In science there are no absolutes.

Another aspect — and it is a different feature — arises from the fact that no experiment, not even the most careful measurement, is free from uncertainty. Throughout the physical sciences, all students are taught to estimate the "probable error" in their measurements. The residual uncertainty in some measurements can be as low as a few parts in a hundred million: even then, no "absolute truth" is available. In Chemistry, the atomic weight of hydrogen is uncertain to a total of fourteen parts in a million: in Physics, one of the most important of all constants, Planck's quantization constant, whose precise value is relevant from astrophysics to the microchip, is uncertain too. Incidentally, it is a well-known fact that scientists, being human and prejudiced in favour of their own best efforts, not so infrequently under-estimate the probable errors in their measurements. Any serious such under-estimates are usually quickly corrected by colleagues.

Even more explicit limitations to the absolute are established in science. A fundamental statement in quatum theory, which governs the atomic world, is what is known as Heisenberg's Uncertainty Principle. This states that there is a definite limit to the precision with which the positions and velocities of atomic particles can be determined. Of course some philosophers, and more theologians, have seized on this theorem to establish the existence of free-will and much else that appeals to them. We need not pursue their wishes, but Heisenberg's Uncertainty Principle is an explicit statement of the widest possible validity that absolute values are unknown to science.

Finally, there is Einstein's Relativity Theory. This, as its name implies, establishes, and in the most general way, that our knowledge of basic features in the physical world (such as the velocities of particles and the times of events) depends upon the frame of reference in which we choose to measure these aspects. Its major consequences are seen in cosmology: but it also shows explicity that no absolute determination of distances or time-intervals is possible.

No-one should imagine that these science aspects are implicit in Gotama's denial of the absolute. All that can be claimed is that whilst whole areas of Graeco-European-Christian philosophy, from Plato onwards, have to be written off as null and void, the open-minded stance of the Tathagata remains valid in the twentieth century.

The congruence between the basic position of Buddhism and modern science deserves two further comments.

It is a striking instance of Gotama's insight: and it lends enormous support to the philosophic outlook he promulgated twenty-five hundred years ago.

Almost equally remarkable is the fact that, despite its humanistic enlightenment, Buddhism cannot claim any substantial role in advancing what might be regarded as scientific studies. Part of this failure, and probably a very large part, must be ascribed to the emphasis in Buddhist teaching on the distress in this world and on the means of escaping it. The Buddhist *sangha* (the community of monks) has always had an essentially monastic character: it represents withdrawal from this world. We shall return to this question.

The open hand and the open mind

The open hand has major significance as a symbol in Buddhism. In the record of his sermons there are several instances of Gotama returning to it. He likened the enlightenment which his teaching aimed to bring to a jewel: the simplicity, directness and conviction which he gave it was that of clear crystal, the value that of a precious gem.

In many of the stories in which the simile of the open hand is used, the emphasis is on the all-important feature that the Tathagata never asked his disciples or his interlocutors to accept conclusions on trust or in faith. He was always prepared to present a reasoned case for his views. Repeatedly he told his companions that he was telling them all he had to say on the question being discussed; he had no wish to hide behind dogmatic statements, and he would deny that such truths as he taught were not the total insight of which he was capable. "The gem is not held in a closed fist: you see it in the palm of my open hand." This figure he used to convince his hearers of the completeness of his message. And the teaching is always characterized as *ehi-passika,* that is "come and see".

Gotama's persuasiveness and effectiveness in debate was such that opponents or doubters, who happened to be well-known public figures, would send one of their supporters or colleagues to question him, rather than risk being worsted in discussion themselves. The Tathagata was well aware of this practice. He treated his serious questioners with marked respect, and often commenced by provisionally accepting their position only to show how, from his vantage point, such an acceptance would have undesirable, if not dire consequences.

The dignity with which he met his opponents rested on the depth and clarity of his own insight. It left an indelible impression on all his hearers. Especially when he would deny even having any special role as leader or head of his monastic order. It was the position of a teacher in a brotherhood that he would claim. This controlled self-effacement is in great contrast to the projections of many other leaders in philosophy and religion. The Tathagata made no claims for himself beyond his possession of enlightenment: a claim he was prepared to demonstrate and a gift he was anxious to share.

Confucius comes to mind as a similar character.

This attitude so impressed Gotama's questioners that many who had come to press their doubts and disbelief would announce their acceptance of his teaching and even ask to join as full disciples. However, if the enquirer was publicly known to be associated with another school, Gotama would usually insist that he remained attached to it until he was quite certain of the need for change.

Who cannot be impressed by the Tathagata's emphasis on the individual finding his own way to the path that he offered and then being free to follow it? There is neither a heavy stick nor a sweet reward to persuade one to conform. Hell is replaced by possible reincarnation, but it is not certain that anyone becomes aware of this. Heaven is replaced by nibbana, a supra-intellectual state of such enlightenment that, at death, one fades out of the universe. Gotama's insistence on the self-determination of the individual was expressed very frequently in many slightly different forms:

> Be ye a refuge to yourselves.
> Look not for a refuge to anyone besides yourselves.
> Be ye lamps unto yourselves.
> Hold fast to the truth as a lamp for your own guidance.
> Hold fast to the truth as a refuge.
> Seek not for any external refuge.
> Good people mould themselves.
> Only by one's own efforts is one purified.

In this position the Tathagata imposed no vows of attachment other than that taken by the monks to pursue without remission the path of the dhamma, i.e., his teaching. Whilst there is a simple solemn ceremony for those entering the sangha (the community of monks) there is no induction for lay followers. They become Buddhists by following Buddha.

The Tathagata's attitude is beautifully illustrated by a story told of his last years. One of his closest disciples, Sariputta, expressed his overwhelming appreciation of the Tathagata:

"Master, I have such faith in the Tathagata that I feel there never has been, nor will there ever be any other teacher greater and wiser than the Buddha". Calmly the answer came: "Your words are impressive and bold, Sariputta: you have burst forth in a song of rapture. But can you believe what you have said?" Notice the reference back to Sariputta: Gotama does not express his own disbelief. Sariputta is brought gently to earth by being reminded that he had little claim to have known all the teachers of the past, and less knowledge of those to come. He should confine himself to what he knows. Why had he gone to such extravagant lengths? He confessed to being carried away and that he only knew "the outline of things".

Gotama is constantly reported as pointing not to himself but to his teaching — "the dhamma is the way". A clear indication of the Tathagata's own stance with relation to his teaching and its limits is enshrined in the challenge brought to him by one of his keenest disciples, Malunkyaputta. This sharp-minded individual saw deficiencies in Gotama's teaching and made a direct approach to his difficulties.

Malunkyaputta approached the Buddha and respectfully explained he was unhappy on many questions which had not been considered in the teaching. What were these questions? Firstly, concerning the universe: was it finite, or infinite, eternal or not eternal? and the soul, how is it differentiated from the body: is there life after death and in what form, if any, does one then exist? (Malunkyaputta's questions were in a more stylized, systematic form, but of the same content.) He explained it was unsatisfactory that these questions (still being asked and debated today — as they will be in the future) had not been considered by the Tathagata. It was not to be expected that, in this uncertainty, he, Malunkyaputta, could remain a disciple if no explanations were forthcoming. Would the Tathagata deal with these questions or honestly admit that he did not know the answers to them?

The Tathagata's answer was very simple, and yet of a maturity which only a minority of teachers up till now have attained.

"Malunkyaputta, is it your case that I have persuaded you to join my disciples and that I would explain these things to you?"

"No, master, that is not so."

"Well then, Malunkyaputta, is it that you have said 'Master, I wish to be a disciple and you shall explain these things to me'"?

"No, master, that is not so."

"So, Malunkyapputta, the position is that neither have I promised to answer these questions, nor have you made it a pre-condition of your becoming a disciple that I should. Accordingly, as far as these questions are concerned, we are each of us free of any obligation."

Then comes the Tathagata's statement of his position.

"If, Malunkyaputta, someone were to tell me he would become a disciple provided I dealt with these questions, then that person would die before the Tathagata had answered them."

"Consider, Malunkyaputta, a man struck by a poisoned arrow which will kill him. He is taken to a surgeon to whom he exclaims: 'I will not allow this arrow to be removed until I know who exactly shot it — of what caste was he, was he a warrior, a priest, a tradesman, or an outcast? What was his name, his family, his appearance? And what type of bow did he use, and how was the arrow made?' Clearly, Malukyaputta, that man would die before his many (interesting but irrelevant) questions were answered? In the same way, anyone, offering your questions for answer as a precondition to accepting my teaching will die before he is answered."

The way to enlightenment, the Tathagata explains, is not to be found by first answering these questions. The right insight comes from firstly appreciating that this life's problems start with birth, and end with death and that much distress will come between them. The "four noble truths" and the eight-fold path must first be grasped.

"Clearly, Malunkyaputta, you must see what I have explained and what I have not explained. I have not dealt with the questions you brought to me. Why so? Because, Malunkyaputta, it is not fundamentally necessary to consider those questions in order to achieve enlightenment. That depends upon accepting the significance and value of the Tathagata's teaching. That is why I have not dealt with your questions."

This is a much abbreviated and re-phrased version of the famous Malukya-sutta (i.e. of the Pali original account of the discourse): but the import is unchanged. Apart from its content, what the reader might also consider is, whether such a realistic presentation of such a sharply discriminating analysis, with its well-defined metaphysical cut-off, could have been invented had it not actually occurred?

This account brings out clearly the assumption in Gotama's teaching that the main need in life is the attainment of enlightenment in the Buddhist sense: that is, an understanding of the character of the human condition and of the means by which its trials can be alleviated. It is also implicit — if not (to my knowledge) explicitly stated — that such enlightenment carries with it a calm acceptance of the human lot. Certainly there is a commitment to improve it in the directions repeatedly — one might say, interminably — emphasized in Gotama's eight-fold path.

This is the assumption of the Buddhist mind, that the Tathagata's teaching will set individuals free from the disillusion and grief they are likely to encounter and that many, but not all, will accept the teaching when they hear it. There is no frantic concern to indoctrinate those who may be indifferent. The supposition is that kamma will inflict rebirth on them until they do achieve enlightenment. In practice, it means the Buddhist advocates the good life essentially for its own value, with the overwhelming sense of composure it will provide. "The peace that passeth all understanding" is rarely represented in the West: it is one of the constant and almost inescapable impressions projected by the benign Buddha figures in the ambience of so many eastern temples.

The dismissal of Malunkyaputta's questions as irrelevant in practice is, from the Tathagata's position, a piece of sound empiricism. Much of the progress in science follows from an abandonment of concern with widely general (the so-called "ultimate") questions, and a concentration on those problems for which a practical analysis can be offered. The aim is to deal with immediately accessible features. After some three centuries of such restricted studies — many of which have been derided in the past for being concerned with the minutiae of things — science is now able to answer *some* of the general questions.

We can now give a very meaningful account of the nature of the sun and the stars and how they influence life on earth, e.g., leaving no slightest shadow of substance in the delusions of astrology. We have a good picture of how the multifarious forms of life have developed on earth. We have a clear insight into the mechanism by which heredity works: etc., etc. The major, ultimate (?) questions have been answered by dealing with problems for which practical procedures could be offered. Gotama's methodology was similar.

"The good life, Malunkyaputta, does not depend upon the question whether the world is or is not eternal, that we are destined for another existence, etc., etc. These hypothetical matters — and others thought up by our busy minds — still leave the problems of life, poverty, failure, disillusion, grief, sickness, old age, untouched. Life itself is scarcely sufficiently long to allow us time to learn how to deal with these trials. When some success has been achieved in coping with them most people will be so imbued with a rewarding sense of freedom that a multitude of hypothetical questions will be seen for what they are — imaginary conundrums."

No god

Buddhism is frequently described as atheistic as it has no place for a supreme controller of the universe. Those most alarmed by this character usually regard the idea of atheism as morally reprehensible. And they have a case. Although they may not always acknowledge it, their fear is that were the absence of a supreme god to be maintained, then there would be no basis for morality in their world and little meaning in the universe. Certainly, the western world had based its ultimate sanctions on the supposed views or wishes of an imaginary Almighty power.

Firstly, let us be clear what Gotama is recorded as saying on this question.

In one context the Tathagata clearly dismisses the beginning of things as beyond our comprehension. This statement is, at least, one of great honesty. He lived in a community provided with a rich mythology of the creation and he was stepping out of line, with perhaps no obvious benefit, in rejecting any such imaginative story.

But there was more to it than that. Even today, most people cannot suspend their judgement or control their wishes in accepting some creator of the universe. Being aware of the universe and its extent in space and time, a compulsion seems to exist to posit a creator. When asked, where does the creator come from, sometimes a meaningless form of words is produced: or, the creator is such as not to need creation: or, the creator is outside the universe observable to humans.

Such replies — and there are far more subtly contrived answers — are not notably clarifying. If the creator needs no creation, why not say the same for the universe? There are, in some quarters, philosophical objections to this possibility. It raises the status of the universe to the self-creating plane. That, it seems, is not appropriate. It does not provide an extra-mundane source of morality, immortality, justice, or whatever else the believer places high in the essentials of human existence. It rather destroys the image of the great father (or mother) figure that most people find very comforting. And the structure (or "design") in the universe "must have been the work of a creator". To which one can at least reply: the universe certainly has a structure: scientists have deduced many aspects which they describe: but the mere existence of a universe necessarily means it will have some form of "structure", even if it were almost a complete chaos. The relevant question is, how does it come to have the structure we observe?

Some readers may recall that in the thirties, a leading theoretician in physics and astronomy, Sir James Jeans, expressed the view that in so far as he could offer any character description, he thought "God must be a mathematician". Jeans may well have felt justified in offering this comment. Philosophers and theologians made great play with it. Jeans himself was a mathematician and there must be some satisfaction in being even in the smallest degree similar to the Almighty. But his serious purpose was to indicate that, from his experience, the universe could only be analyzed and adequately represented in mathematical terms: then, if at all describable, the Almighty appeared to have created the universe on a mathematical ground-plan.

Jeans himself would have been the first to admit the dangers of accepting this as more than a picturesque comment. One qualification is that, of the comprehended universe, both on the largest and smallest scales, including many aspects of life processes, huge areas are dominated by the calculus of probabilities. It follows, that if the Almighty is a mathematician, then he has a strong streak of the gambler.

Few modern theologians would claim they have any clear proof of the existence of God, and those who do, reveal the parlous weakness of their position in the quality of the supposed proof. The more usual position is to argue that our human life has adequate meaning (for which meaning, of course, only human views are available), or that the theist's mind is less unhappy, or that mankind can only be lifted above the level of "the brute creation", only if the existence of a Power outside the observable universe is accepted.

It is of restricted significance to quote any opinions in so speculative an area, but one response to the limitation of the usual view of the Almighty was expressed by Einstein.*

> "Common to all these types is the anthropomorphic character of their conception of God. Only individuals of exceptional endowments and exceptionally high-minded communities, as a general rule, get in any real sense beyond this level. . . .
> The individual feels the nothingness of human desires and aims and the sublimity and marvellous order which reveal themselves both in nature and in the world of thought . . . The beginnings of cosmic religious feeling already appear in earlier stages of development . . . Buddhism, as we have learnt from the wonderful writings of Schopenhauer especially, contains a much stronger element of it."

Watching the scene for a mere fifty years convinces one of how extremely hazardous it is even to suggest any final appraisal of the universe from the views attained at any one date. Astronomy, as much as any other branch of science, has gone through an astonishing expansion, both qualitative and quantitative, in the last fifty years. At the end of the twentieth century the situation shows perhaps a greater flux of novelties than ever previously. Not that major advances have not been adequately established (e.g. the mechanisms by which the stars acquire their energies): but no-one can justifiably imagine that

---

*The World as I See It.
John Lane Bodley Head, 1935, pp.25–26

any certainty on the *modus operandi* of the creation and evolution of the universe can yet be achieved.

Thus far I have been commenting on the views of scientists in the not-so-recent past. What is the situation as we approach the end of the twentieth century? In facing that question, a major difficulty is encountered. Modern physics and modern cosmological theories can scarcely be presented in simple terms, and certainly not safely by one (like myself) not expertly qualified in these areas. However, the lay-scientist can grasp important elements in the situation.

With the extension of particle-physics studies to energy values of truly enormous values, and of astronomical observations to limits previously unexplored, a host of new, frequently bizarre results have appeared. Especially in the astronomical field, these results provide a fascinating thrill by their very strangeness, but it should be remembered that that, in itself, is no criterion of their significance. Fundamental is the fact that the representation of many of these new features can only adequately be given in mathematical terms, and, very frequently, the mathematics is of such an abstruse character that its "meaning", i.e. its description in verbal terms, is highly problematic. The uncertainty which is often an element of these special areas of modern science would seem to provide an ideal free-for-all ground for god-seekers, and a whole host of wallowers in mysticism. And they are taking full advantage of it.

In particle-physics, the departure from the traditional 'simplicity' of what one can call Newtonian concepts, can be taken to start with the neutrino: and now we also have charm, colour, strangeness, quarks, gluon, etc. All these entities are expressions of structural or behavioural aspects of what are currently regarded as 'fundamental' particles. They have little significant meaning when divorced from their mathematical representations.

In astronomy we have the big-bang, pulsars, quasars, black-holes, and string-theories. All are richly spiced components for highly speculative brews.

As it is impossible for me to pursue these recondite modern aspects, let me offer the reader some guidance to sources where expositions can be found. An immediately relevant account is given by William Poundstone's *The Recursive Universe: Cosmic*

Complexity and the Limits of Scientific Knowledge, Oxford University Press, 1987. This book was considered for the Pulitzer prize, and so its contents are very largely accessible to the lay reader.

Then there is Paul Davies's *God and the New Physics*, Penguin Books, 1984. It seems not unreasonable to suggest that my namesake is both a Pythagorean (as was Eddington) and a Spinozan — in his popular writings he is intent on finding God in his astronomical studies, and he is fascinated by large numbers. More significant is his emphasis on the numerical values for physical constants which *appear* to be carefully chosen so as to allow the universe to escape from a catastrophic instablity. This "God deduced from numbers" has become a favoured syndrome to replace the "God of the gaps" — i.e. one invoked on the basis that science (or reason) cannot explain everything. This need to have an explanation for everything is a truly infantile condition. In view of the enormous scale of the universe, from subatomic particles, through viruses and humans, to clusters of extra-galactic nebulae, who but a simpleton can imagine that our brains, operating on these systems for a mere three hundred years, are likely to achieve anything approaching an understanding of it all?

Finally, there is Stephen Hawking's *A Brief History of Time*, Bantam Press, 1988. This has been rightly and widely acclaimed as an exposition of the mathematical modelling of the forces which the human mind currently finds it necessary to postulate in describing the universe. Incidentally, it disposes of the basis for some of the God-fixing by numbers which appeals to Professor Paul Davies and many others. What is called 'the chaotic inflationary model' of the universe accounts, inter alia, for the precise rate of its observed expansion, and gives not only the correct background of astronomical microwave energy, but also a reasonable estimate for the fluctuations found in its value.

I cannot do better than offer three quotations from *A Brief History of Time:*

> p.136: Hawking does his best to explain a currently favoured proposal that the totality of space-time can be finite but unbounded. Insofar as that will survive further developments: "The universe would be completely self-

> contained and not affected by anything outside itself. It would just BE."
>
> p.139: "... a scientific theory is just a mathematical model we make to describe our observations: it exists only in our minds. So it is meaningless to ask: Which is real ...? It is simply a matter of which is the more useful description.' ("Useful" here means "effective in representing observations.")
>
> p.x: From Carl Sagan's Introduction:
> "This is also a book about God ... or perhaps about the absence of God. ... Hawking is attempting, as he explicitly states, to understand the mind of God. And this makes all the more unexpected the conclusion of the effort, at least so far: a universe with no edge in space, no beginning or end in time, and nothing for a Creator to do."

Cognate to these appraisals is the fact that apologists for religion who still retain an attachment to dogma — and Clifford Longley The Times Religious Affairs editor is one such — are quick to point out that modern theoretical physics often presents a dogmatic approach. This arises from its frequent procedure of postulating *a priori* a scheme of things and then deducing mathematically, consequences which conform to at least some major observations. In The Times of March 25, 1989 Mr Longley confidently presents the demise of secularism in a sharply focussed commentary, "Inquest on the Enlightenment." I quote: "If science and secular philosophy rest on assumptions no more nor less secure than religious faith and of the same (not, be it noted, "perhaps of similar") dogmatic character, then ... religion need no longer cringe in the corner."

Of course, this "if" clause most definitely does not apply. But what is of general significance here is that any dogmatic assertions made in the science field will only last as long as experimental evidence supports them. When negated by observational data, they are abandoned. Not so in religion, where dogma remains dogma. Mr Longley's attempted deduction is patently false: on its basis and on his suppositions, religion, if it ever did, can remain "cringeing in the corner."

To summarise: one significant step has been taken in the last decade. The possibility has been seen of constructing a cosmology such that the universe will necessarily have the structure and history that observations suggest. The problem, it seems, is to find what, in simple terms, can be called the correct geometry for the space-time continuum. Insights into this modelling of the cosmos suggest that this self-reference system may well be achieved. (Sakharov, the dissident Russian scientist, has been one of those actively pursuing the question). Obviously, this is not the place to attempt an account of an extraordinary advance in our human effort at describing the universe. But the possibility appears that there could be a meaning to the expression that the universe created itself.

We have wandered from Buddhism? No; we have merely shown how intuitively wise Gotama was in denying any knowledge of a creator. That opinion essentially coincides with the restrained views of those perhaps best qualified by their study of the universe to express an opinion.

Gotama gave other reasons for rejecting the concept of an all-powerful god. Such a being is almost invariably given the status of law-giver both in the physical and moral worlds. God is not only the ultimate reference in establishing what is good and ill, but he (she) arranges that those responsible for deeds of different characters shall be rewarded or punished. The Judaeo-Christian-Moslem world is committed to this view. Not, it seems, universally so. One prominent Christian apologist, the Rev. Don Cupitt, dean of Emmanuel College, Cambridge "reduces it (the Christian religion) to faith alone, far more literally than Luther ever did. It is not faith in anything, just a choice to try to be a certain kind of person, which he aptly calls a kind of Buddhist." (*The Times*, September 17, 1984). Another highly regarded philosopher and Christian apologist has been equally frank in attempting to characterize the Ultimate. Professor H. D. Lewis writes (in *World Religions*, Watts & Co. Ltd., London, 1966) that the insistence on transcendence (i.e. of entities, such as God, which are outside this world) amounts to an insistence on *absolute mystery*. If words have their usual meaning, that is an insistence on something which not only cannot be encountered, but cannot be described. "It can but lead to an exceedingly mischievous glorification of unreason." (Lewis, loc.cit.). This glorification of unreason has, through the centuries, been endemic in Christianity and it has occupied an enormous place in Mahayana Buddhism. Gotama favoured a simpler view. He regarded kamma — the law of cause and effect — as an inherent part of the nature of the universe. No extra-mundane authority metes out punishment to the ill-doer. The quality of the deed carries its own consequences. This does not seem a convincing picture in practice. Too many scoundrels get away with murder in this world, and the few saints often appear to go unrewarded. But we must remember that the Tathagata was convinced of the cycle of rebirths. Those who get away with murder in one incarnation would (for Gotama) suffer the inevitable consequences of their deeds in a later incarnation. It is clear that the cycle of rebirth is essential to the Buddhist appraisal of the evils in this world. It provides an all-embracing schema which can account for the dreadful vagaries which life on earth exhibits: the frightful poverty, distress, and pain visited on so many who seem to have done nothing to deserve the fate they suffer: and conversely also for so many in the lap of luxury. The rebirth hypothesis offers some possible understanding of these discrepancies but it is baseless. So the problem remains. It is given equally fictitious solutions in other philosophical and religious systems. Perhaps the question to be tackled is why should we expect the world to offer what we would call justice?

Throughout his teaching the Tathagata carefully avoided the transcendental: he offered no credence to imagined influence from some other world. Although it did not originate with Gotama, Buddhist sources imply the universe evolved naturally (i.e. as a consequence of the inherent character of its content) from matter dispersed through cosmic space. No act of creation is suggested. This absence of creation was essentially an element in 'Indian' thought which, before Gotama's time, generally accepted a cyclical pattern for the universe in time. To those who suggested to Gotama that a Supreme Being was involved in over-seeing human affairs he was unusually dismissive. "So then, thanks to this Creator, men become murderers, thieves, unchaste, liars, malicious and perverse in their minds. If one believes in the existence of a Supreme Being who organizes the world, then there is neither desire nor reason for doing this deed or for abstaining from that. The

Creator is always ultimately responsible."

Not only did the Tathagata reject the supernatural, he strongly opposed metaphysical speculation. When questioned on the creation of the universe he averred it was meaningless to speculate on such remotely conceivable events. It produced only "the jungle, the desert, the writhing, the entanglement of speculation . . . conducing neither to wisdom nor to insight." Many will feel that he was avoiding an issue and claim that this is where God must come in. But if asked how or when God was created, the answer would be "God has no beginning: did not need to be created." This is the classic *deus ex machina* syndrome. The inability to explain the origin of the universe is translated into an inability to explain the origin of God. It is an interesting facet of a mind that it is unhappy not knowing how the visible, much experienced universe arose, and is relieved by transferring the not-knowing to an entity for whose existence the only evidence is its own imagination.

In one commentary on Gotama's dismissal of metaphysics it is claimed that the Pali records have some sixty-two questions on the Supreme Being: the soul: the eternity of the creation: the reason for the creation: etc. All these questions the Tathagata refused to answer. It was not an oversight but a deliberate choice not to speculate on questions of which we have no experience.

By the credibility of so many individuals, one is frequently reminded of "*Credo quia absurdum est*": I believe because it is ridiculous.

The unity of the world

The physical cosmology depicted in classical Buddhist texts is entirely fictional. The world is a scene of mountains and plains surrounded by water. This picture, like much else in the early sources, is derived from or shared with the contemporaneous Hindu teachings. Likewise derived is the idea of a plurality of worlds or universes. The latter term is appropriate as these systems are envisaged as persisting for enormous periods of time but, nevertheless, themselves going through cycles of destruction, reformation, persistence, decay and destruction.

The whole of this cosmology is mythological; but its general character is significant. At no stage is it imagined that this earth is a special creation or the centre of the universe. And the vast time scale gives a background of great freedom to Hindu and Buddhist thought. Whilst it is an accidental coincidence, these two major aspects — the plurality of worlds and the great periods of their duration — find close similarities in our present knowledge. Not only are there hundreds of millions of galaxies (or "island universes"), but their age is of the order of ten thousand million years. Strictly, we know of only one universe: everything that is observable is within it. No practical meaning can be attached to "outside the universe", as that implies that no observation or information can be acquired from such inconceivable a region. However, it does offer scope for some philosophers to speculate.

This Buddhist cosmology is in marked contrast to Greek and Near-Eastern views which filtered into and dominated European thought for so long. Perhaps the truly parochial cosmology having the world as its centre was culturally determined by Egyptian and Mesopotamian civilizations, developing, as those civilizations did, within the narrow confines of river valleys surrounded by deserts.

The Buddhist outlook is inherently on a world-wide scale. Two aspects have already been mentioned. The enlightenment achieved by the Tathagata is confidently accepted as amply adequate for all other worlds. The basis for such confidence is its claim to represent the truth. It is also clearly assumed that other worlds will, fundamentally, be constructed and share the same pattern as ours.

Toynbee and others have emphasized that monotheistic societies have, in the West, elevated man to a position, if not above nature then to a supreme status within nature. The traditional Christian view, almost universally held within the Church until well into this century, has been that the universe was created to display the salvation of men on earth. This depressed the whole of the non-human world to a secondary, merely supportive or decorative role. Man was put in a privileged commanding position. The enormity of this astonishing assumption of human uniqueness was undoubtedly appreciated by Pascal and led to one of his many memorable expressions: *Le silence eternel des éspaces infinites m'effraye.*

Many can abandon the imaginative figments of the virgin

birth and the corporeal resurrection, but it is difficult to see how even the Bishop of Durham can disclaim this world was created so that men's souls may be saved without, that is, forsaking all semblance of traditional Christianity.

In Hindu and Buddhist thought the whole universe, and man in it, are one indivisible whole. Although derived from a primitive animistic picture of the world, when expressed in the elevated terms of the Vedas and Buddhist doctrine, this view provided powerful restraints on man's impulse to indulge his greed against others and at the expense of the non-human environment.

Now the Greeks arrived at insights of extraordinary depth and validity by their development of logical reasoning. Their supreme achievements are in mathematics. Buddhist philosophy seems to have arrived at major conclusions by intuitive insight. The conclusion that there are many other worlds of the same character as ours would seem to be essentially correct. We shall come to some substantial limitations to this conclusion, but, in general terms the whole vast universe is constructed from the same forms of matter and energy as we encounter on earth. Life, in any form presently conceivable to us, cannot occur far outside the temperature range we find it surviving in here. The whole of our current knowledge of material systems suggests that processes necessarily as intricate as those in living organisms can only take place in an aqueous environment. Water appears essential to life. Normally it exists as a liquid only from 0° to 100°C, but life persists beyond these limits.

It would be ridiculous to suggest that the Buddhist conception of life on other worlds conforms to our present limited understanding. What is truly significant is that the Buddhist outlook is in no way embarrassed by the possible discovery of life, and intelligent life at that, in other worlds. Philosophies allocating a unique role to this world are in a different boat, itself subject to irreversible leaking: apart, that is, from the probability of its already having sunk without trace.

The earlier statement that matter and energy throughout the universe take the same forms as on earth needs major qualification in terms of the newer astronomy. Neutron stars, quasars, and black holes are some material states only imagined within recent years. Despite their great significance cosmologically, it is improbable that they contribute anything which is essential for life processes.

Buddhism, we see, accepts the universe as a unity. It also, almost necessarily, accepts this world as unitary. This viewpoint is beautifully clear: "No dividing line can be drawn between the man, the tree, and the mountain." If it offered nothing else, the Buddhist outlook would deserve acclaim for this alone.

The exclusion of any sharp qualitative differentation between the mineral, the biological, and the human is a remarkable insight to have been intuitively grasped twenty-five hundred years ago. It is a not unacceptable synopsis of what twentieth century science suggests. A critical approach necessarily asks whether it was not, perhaps, just a lucky shot in the dark, or a lucky guess? The answer is, no. The statement encapsulates in a brilliant phrase the continuity of existence that Gotama accepted as a picture of the world.

Again, it is a view derived from the corpus of early Indian thought. Its acceptance in Buddhist teaching acquires special significance in that this thesis is accepted in a rational context. It is not the result of some mystical insight: nor is it decorated with fantastic legends. At least, not in the Theravada canon. In some Mahayana teachings, and especially in Tantric excursions, a whole panoply of spirits is available to support the idea.

The contrast with generally better known philosophies need not be pursued. Spinoza, it might be claimed, put the world he knew of on a unitary basis. His God was in everything, producing an all-pervading pantheism. He achieved a high degree of consistency by also applying an universal cloak of mysticism.

But is the Buddhist dictum true? Well, it is a good approximation to such truth as we have attained. Between man and the tree the bridge has been provided by the geological record of life on earth and the establishment of the evolutionary pattern. This "establishment" does not necessitate the acceptance of the theory of evolution (i.e. the explanation of *how* the development occurred), but rather the acceptance of the observations *that it has occured*. The record suffices to show (and one approaches the flat-earth category if one denies) that all life on earth has gradually developed over hundreds of millions of years from the simplest possible initial organisms. In that context one can trace back the path of life, in general terms, to a point shared in common by man and the tree. David Attenborough's T.V. presentation of "*Life on Earth*" provided a brilliant, illustrated exposé of this thesis.

The unity of all forms of life is a fact of palaeontology. The unity of the living and non-living in the sense that (*vide,* the Buddhist dictum) no sharp line can be drawn between them, is a result observed following on the work of Wendell Stanley (1935). One of the simplest forms of life of which we humans are only too well aware are the viruses — they give us, *inter alia,* influenza, chicken pox, poliomyelitis, and the common cold. They are very much alive in the sense accepted for simple organisms — they multiply rapidly in appropriate media and they thrive, to pass from one cell to another, in those organs which they infect.

Virus behaviour in plant diseases has given the clearest picture of their character. The tobacco-mosaic virus (tmv) is recognized by the patchy colour it imparts to tobacco leaves, and it is fatal to their normal growth. This was one of the earliest viruses to be isolated. It can be purified so adequately that it crystallizes out as a reproducibly pure material. As such, it can be kept indefinitely without further change, either of growth or of deterioration. It can be dissolved in water and there behaves like a chemical compound of well-defined character, rather precisely defined by constant size and shape. Its molecular weight is that of a large polymer species (which is its physico-chemical description) having a value near 40 million units. Its long cylindrical form is so well defined and so constant that it is used to calibrate the magnification of electron microscopes. And yet this non-living molecule returns to life, and reproduces itself, as soon as it is put in a medium with suitable nutrients. The reversible transformation, living $\leftrightarrow$ dead, can be achieved for tmv as frequently as the experimenter wishes.

This is the sort of evidence (there is a great volume of it) that suggests there is no insurmountable barrier between living and dead material. This does not mean that any material can somehow be made alive. It means that there is nothing in living material which is not present in dead material other than an appropriate complexity of structure and specificity of character which results in the appearance of life. In tmv the whole pattern of organization is retained in the crystalline state, which is no longer alive because it has no material to feed on or to reproduce itself. And it can be kept indefinitely before being returned to "life".

Thus the "breath of life" is essentially the result of an adequately complex organic structure with a suitably specific reactivity. Sixty years ago it was still possible for some biologists to argue that a special "vital force" was needed to explain the staggeringly intricate pattern of events which characterizes living organisms. Such "vitalists" are now in almost the same category as the flat-earthers.

A hundred and sixty years ago it was thought by chemists that the organic compounds then found in living organisms, or produced by living organisms, as alcohol is produced by yeast, could themselves only be generated thanks to the "vital force" in the living process. Iron oxide, copper sulphide, calcium carbonate (marble, chalk), sandstone, were well recognized minerals or rocks, and were (and are) described as inorganic materials: urea, acetic acid (vinegar), alcohol, quinine, etc. were produced by living organisms, and, it was originally thought, could only be so produced. But, in the laboratory, it was found that these organic compounds could be produced from inorganic materials, that is from substances which were of purely mineral origin. The vital force was not needed, and it promptly disappeared from chemistry. Thus there is no insurmountable barrier between the inorganic materials of the mountain and the organic materials which make up the tobacco mosaic virus or those which make up the tree.

It may be thought that special pleading has been introduced in thus bridging the apparent gaps between the man, the tree, and the mountain. The pleading is in no way special. The examples cited have necessarily been so, as it was appropriate to quote simple instances. The position can be easily categorized. If anyone thinks there is a significant qualitative barrier between the man, the tree, and the mountain, then he should inform the biologists and chemists where this is, as these scientists have not found it in any of their studies.

The unity sketched above has been in terms of the material constituents and the properties they confer on the various systems they form. Many thinkers feel this is too crude an assessment: they claim that something more, something unexpected arises when simpler units (atoms, molecules, cells, etc.) come together to form larger structures. In 1931 the centenary meeting of the British Association was presided over by one of the few major figures to emerge from South Africa, General Jan Smuts. His appearance on the science stage arose from his exposition of what were thought (by some) to be the limitations in the synopsis of the "materialist" thesis given above. He was a protagonist of the philosophical theory of holism. This theory accepts that the world is made up from basic units: the atoms from nuclear particles, all materials from atoms, all living organism from component atom-containing molecules, etc. Holism claims that at each stage of the aggregation of smaller units to larger structures, entirely new properties appear which are not present or even implied by the character of the simpler individual units. It is argued that essentially new features emerge, thanks to cooperative interactions within the aggregates; these emergent properties, it is claimed, cannot be foreseen in the character of the component units and, moreover, they are of a higher status than any properties shown by the units. In particular, life has aspects which cannot be deduced from the behaviour of its constituent parts, and humans, representing the most advanced or highly developed form of life, exhibit features unknown in lower organisms. This plausible picture allows, inter alia, of the ascription of unique, e.g., 'spiritual', values to humans.

Philosophers, it seems, have been generally unimpressed by the holistic thesis. There are three good reasons for commenting on it here. Firstly, through recorded history reason has had to fight its way forward against successive entrenchments of obscurantism or mysticism. Those who do not appreciate the extraordinary subtlety of even the simplest material systems (e.g., as seen in the behaviour of atoms) and those who, for wider and deeper reasons, wish to reject a materialist view of the world, such thinkers always seize on what to them is an unexplained aspect of experience and build their intellectual castles from clouds of uncertainty. Holism is such a castle. Secondly, having been dormant for some fifty years, the holistic view is being refurbished to establish, if possible, that "there is a mind behind the universe". Thirdly, were this so, Buddhism would be seriously deficient in not recognizing it.

One does not need to be a Buddhist to reject holism. The progress of knowledge and reasoned analysis suffices. That holism is, in essence, based on ignorance is clear by reference to the features firmly planted in its presentation sixty years ago.

What was then an apparently convincing case came as follows. Hydrogen and oxygen atoms are built of positive nuclei and negative electrons: these atoms form molecules (H_2 and O_2). The individual atom, the molecules they form, and especially the gases formed by aggregates of the molecules have remarkably different properties from their constituent parts — "in no way implied or deducible from the properties of sub-atomic particles". These gases combine chemically to form a new molecule, H_2O, the unique component particle of water vapour, aggregates of which in turn form drops of liquid water, a medium of remarkable properties "in no way related to the properties of the gases from which it was formed". The properties of the gases, and later, those of liquid water, have emerged from those of their constituent particles where they were in no way inherent.

The facts in these instances have not changed but the holistic deductions have now been most specifically eliminated.

It is a measure of the advances of physical science that we now understand and can calculate quantitatively

(i) how the nuclei and electrons interact to form atoms having the known properties of the H and O atoms;

(ii) how these atoms combine to form H_2 and O_2 molecules of the observed size, large numbers of which have the properties found for their gases (viscosity, etc.) and even the boiling points of their liquids;

(iii) how the H and O atoms combine to form the H_2O molecule with its known geometrical structure and physical properties:

(iv) how these H_2O molecules interact to produce a liquid having the special structure and properties of water in bulk.

All chemistry graduands now learn these evaluations in terms of well defined quantum-theoretical models. The whole is derived from the interaction of electrons with nuclei and with themselves. The treatment is sufficiently precise to have revealed some aspects of water behaviour not previously grasped.*

This particular instance shows how the "emergent" properties, not seen in the constituents, prove to be a necessary consequence of the subtle natures of the component particles. Thanks to quantum mechanics applied with the help of modern computers, the "higher status" aspects are deduced from the inferior parts. For many other gaps in our understanding, claimed by the holists for "emergent elements", similar clarification has not yet arrived: nor may it do so, perhaps for several centuries. Analytical science is only some four hundred years old: our world has been developing its intricacies for about four thousand million years. For the foreseable future there will be ample scope for holists and others anxious to exploit the unknown to work up "mysteries" and to deduce the presence of "unknown movers". Only a simpleton can imagine that mankind should so soon have found all the answers. We must learn to live, as the scientist does, with uncertainty. We should not base our outlook on areas of ignorance. Few of Gotama's messages were more constantly reiterated than: ignorance is the source of much delusion.

We return from the digression on holism to the picture of the unitary world of science.

It should not be imagined that there is any shadow of a suggestion that Buddhist teaching anticipated, in more than spirit, this unified picture of the world we live in. But it is to the credit of the Tathagata that he refused to divide humans from their fellow creatures, or these from the rest of the world. It is a result of the profound appreciation that Gotama formed, that the individual is an indissoluble part or product of his environment, and that his experiences and behaviour cannot be separated from it except by introducing arbitrary categories.

This indissoluble link arises from a full acceptance of the

*Many readers will see from this instance that Chemistry as a science has been transformed in the last fifty years. As initiated by Lavoisier and Dalton it was a qualitative, descriptive, empirical account of atoms and molecules (which, however, acquired substantial slices of sound mathematico-physical theory). It has now been firmly based on fundamental aspects of quantum theory and this allows the properties of atoms and molecules to be calculated from the characters of their constituent particles.

individual's situation as seen by the Tathagata. No external powers are involved to account for the situation. There is no authority beyond the natural world anxious to impart or suggest patterns of behaviour to the individual. The idea of sin, taken as a breaking of rules or patterns of behaviour derived from a supra-mundane source, is completely alien to Buddhism.

In one important respect only, it seems, does Gotama distinguish the human from the remainder of the living world. Only humans can achieve enlightenment. He does not seem to have reached the position of St. Francis who preached to the birds. However, the Buddhist has traditionally treated his fellow creatures with deliberate respect. An interesting recognition of this came when that remarkable Christian, Dr. Albert Schweitzer, announced his guiding principle as "reverence for life": he was quickly described as "not so much a Christian as a Buddhist". What is universally accepted throughout all forms of Buddhism is that no creature should be cruelly treated.

The question of vegetarianism has already been mentioned. Occasions are certainly described in the Theravada record in which Gotama accepted meat when he was the guest of non-Buddhists. The explanation offered is that he was not responsible for the killing which must have occurred. Many Buddhists appear to accept that, provided no cruelty has been inflicted in maintaining the animals (chickens, cows, pigs, etc.), and that none ocurs in their slaughter, then meat eating is not necessarily forbidden, but in many communities vegetarianism is highly regarded.

Only in the very rarest instances will a committed Buddhist be found to be responsible for the slaughter of animals. To indulge in such killing virtually rules one out of the Buddhist community. On this prohibition Spiro has written: "Like Hinduism, the parent religion, Buddhism interdicts the killing of all beings . . . Unlike Hinduism, however, the Buddhist interdiction stems not so much from the Hindu notion of non-violence (*ahimsa*), but from its own concept of *metta,* or loving-kindness. *Metta,* for Buddhism, is the noblest of all sentiments, it is the mark of the truly moral man. From the Buddhist point of view, the taking of any form of life is a denial of *metta* and is accounted as murder."

It is noticeable that the line drawing (i.e. on meat eating) is not done dogmatically: the element of reason in relation to cruelty is allowed to operate. The absence of the absolute in this approach is instructive and, perhaps, also appealing to those without prejudice.

The question of our relations with the animal world has come in for much public attention in recent years. Many occasions arise where the elimination of vermin or dangerous creatures becomes a practical necessity. The Buddhist would not object to this being done provided there is a minimum infliction of suffering. The possibility of such activity becoming a pleasure or sport, as in fox-hunting, would be unthinkable to a Buddhist. The Judaeo-Christian-Moslem tradition is entirely different. Spain, one of the most Christian of countries, has a notorious record of cruelty to animals. Such practices as bull-fighting, cock-fighting, bear-baiting, were originally condoned by the all-powerful church as, unlike their tormentors, animals are not possessed of Christian souls. Unfortunately, the treatment meted out to animals was easily carried over to humans and this, it seems, was justifiable when the humans were not of the same Christian belief as that which dominated in Spain. The histories of the Spanish Inquisition, of the nineteenth century Peninsular War, and of the Spanish Civil War in this century provide only too much evidence of nauseating behaviour.

One further aspect of the unity of the world must be considered. It implies, and the Tathagata many times preached and demonstrated, that no barriers must be raised on a basis of class, or poverty, or race, or sex. The status of women in Buddhism requires a special comment which comes later. Here we can deal with the other categories.

The caste-system of the Hindus, not fully established in the time of the Tathagata, was alien to him. He was not blind to the differences between individuals, nor to the fact that some are capable of far higher achievements in this life than others. His picture of the lotuses emerging to different degrees from the water is an excellent simile. He frequently showed his disciples, in practice and precept, that the teacher must adjust his level to that appropriate to his pupils: only few would be in a position to grasp the full light of his message, but none would be unable to derive some benefit from it. In terms of poverty or caste, the much quoted instance of Gotama accepting the street-sweeper, Sunita, into the order of monks without hesitation, tells all that need be said. Domestic servants were given by Gotama the same reception as princes. Even those who were in the position of slaves were accepted as neophytes provided they were first released from serfdom. That freedom was to be sought from their master. Such an unbiased approach to his fellow humans reflects the huge confidence of the Tathagata in the universal relevance of his message and of his full acceptance of the brotherhood of men.

Women in Buddhism

The status of women in the Buddhist community bears little resemblance to the place they occupied in Western religions. In these latter, they were scarcely tolerated in any active role. St. Paul showed his bias when he categorized them.* Several of the fathers of the Christian church described women in terms too completely abusive to be quoted. This view was principally based on the sexual temptations they presented to men. The bias so injected has not yet been eliminated in many areas of the Western world. Apart from the Church of Rome, perhaps the Church of England will be one of the last upholders of statutory discrimination against women.

The accounts of Gotama's relations with women will carry, for some readers, a strong impression of reality: when considered in relation to the poor status of women in the communities in which he lived, they certainly are not of a character which suggests they were invented. Nor were they chosen for popular appeal: rather they show a conviction for equality of the sexes, although this was, in practice, greatly qualified. However, the historicity of the initial induction of women as monks has been challenged. There are, too, stories in the literature of Gotama warning his disciples of the wiles of women and speaking of their supposed weaknesses. As he very rarely spoke ill of anyone and he insisted that each individual must be considered in the light of his/her own merits and defects, these accounts are probably apocryphal, that is, later

---

* 1st Epistle to the Corinthians, Chapter XI:

Verse 7: For the man . . . is the image and glory of God: but the woman is the glory of the man.

Verse 9: Neither was the man created for the woman; but the woman for the man.

inventions the better to conform with common prejudice.

When it was suggested to Gotama, twenty-five hundred years ago, that women should be admitted to the sangha, he at first firmly refused the suggestion: and, the record says, he persisted in his rejection for some time. Recalling that commitment to the priesthood involved abandoning one's family, he concluded that it would be inappropriate for women to do this. The Theravada sources, in what seems convincingly real detail, report that, amongst others, the Tathagata's favourite disciple, Ananda, pressed him to reconsider his decision. Eventually he responded to this pressure, and accepted that women should form their own order alongside that of the monks.

The traditional story has it that Gotama had spent some ten years happily married to a beautiful young wife. He himself emphasized what a wrench it was when he decided he must leave home in his search for enlightenment. This experience would have profoundly influenced his outlook. Being fully aware of the range of sensuality, its emotions and practices, he never made the appalling mistake of indentifying sex with sin, but he was in no doubt as to the temptations it presented. It was, perhaps, his realization of the greater involvement in, and attachment to, the home which women traditionally display, that gave him cause to doubt whether the state of homelessness, which was emphasized in the monk's entering the priesthood, was appropriate for women.

As Buddhist monks are committed to celibacy, there was no possibility of the women joining the some temples or monasteries as men. They were, however, allowed an entirely similar separate, organized, order which, like the men's, would be entirely democratic. The nuns wuld elect their own head-of-house from amongst their number. In many important respects, the abbess would be merely *prima-inter-pares*, the first amongst equals. The rules for the conduct of the nuns exactly paralleled those for the monks, but they were, however, to be in substantial degree, subservient to the monks. Nuns and monks were to meet at fortnightly intervals for recitation of the rules of conduct and for consideration of any problems which the nuns might have. The monks were to be consulted if any problems did arise in the nunnery and the monks' collective opinion, in any case of dispute, was to be finally binding.

Inferior though this status was, it provided for a full commitment by women to the path of enlightenment.

Gotama's concern for what he clearly regarded as the greater strain on women joining the Sangha appears in his ruling that whilst the minimum probationary period for men joining the priesthood was four months, for women this period was two years before they could be fully inducted. This provided the neophyte with ample time to find whether she was happy to make a final break with the everyday world.

The rules for the nuns were parallel to those for the monks. A detailed set of rules had been spelt out for the activities of the monks and were applied equally to the nuns: the times at which they should rise, wash, eat, meditate, meet for recitation (later also reading) of the doctrine, etc. A strict code of behaviour was stipulated, but no penances or punishments were established for lapses or misdeeds. Such details and day-to-day items were to be decided by the consensus view of the monks and nuns of each house. Unruly individuals were faced with the ultimate sanction of expulsion.

Gotama clearly had reservations in agreeing to what was necessarily a separate organization for women disciples. He told Ananda that, in the absence of the institution of the nuns, he expected the Buddhist teaching to survive for a thousand years. In view of his firm confidence in the supreme value of the enlightenment which he had achieved and of the wide acceptance and great commitment which his teachings had acquired, this period of a thousand years reflects the modesty and realism of the Tathagata. However, he averred that the separate establishment of the nuns would reduce this effective lifetime of his teaching from a thousand to five hundred years. An intriguing pessimistic judgement, completely negated by history.

H. C. Warren in the commentary within his volume *Buddhism in Translation* (Harvard University Press, 1922) writes that there were few, if any, Buddhist nuns in Sri Lanka at the start of this century. There appears to have been a gap between possibilities and actual practice in this respect. We shall return to this question.

Gotama, the records suggest, always treated women with much consideration and respect. On one notable occasion, he accepted an invitation to himself and his disciples to a meal with a rich courtesan. This, again, does not seem a story likely to have been invented. Undoubtedly the Tathagata had complete confidence in being able to turn aside any temptations which might arise. The meal is described as rich, if not sumptuous, and the courtesan is said to have engaged in discussion as to the teaching, of which she had heard many reports. The upshot was, one version says, that she herself undertook to follow the Buddhist path.

In another context there is the account of the Tathagata meeting the ruler of Kosala. The latter was distressed (as would have been usual for a person in his circumstances) by the news that his wife had presented him with a daughter. Gotama is described as making light of the king's dissatisfacion, which he countered by insisting "that some women are superior to men".

It can always be queried whether this account relates to an actual incident. The question is of no great relevance. Buddhists have accepted it as reflecting the views of their teacher and have generally acted accordingly. *Verb. sap.*

In the same category is the account of Gotama's return, at his father's request, to his home at Kapilàvastu. His fame was already widespread and he was attended by many disciples. The family and members of his father's retinue came to meet him and paid their respects to the Tathagata. All except the mother of his son, Yasodhara. She refused to go to her husband, saying that if she had any virtue he would come to her. This he did, taking two of his disciples with him. Yasodhara was so overcome, she knelt at his feet and kissed them.

The story at least symbolizes the recurring impression that Gotama never put himself on a pedestal. He always made a simple, calm, direct approach to any problem he encountered.

The origin of enlightenment

In earlier sections outlining the four noble truths and the eight-fold path, these aspects of the Tathagata's teaching have been spelt out directly; that is, they are taken as providing their own justification. However, Buddhist thought is not satisfied with such simplicity. An extensive philosophy and metaphysics has been developed as a basis to the teaching. I would not claim that anything is gained by the system so evolved. It does, however, embody much of the background of historic Buddhist ideas and, whilst no better justified than other conceptual systems, certain aspects carry, I think, their own value. The following synopsis is, at best, a bare outline of much subtle speculation.

The pattern of ideas seems to start from Gotama's enunciation of *dukkha* as the widespread, if not universal, feeling of dissatisfaction in human life, and its origin in unfulfilled wishes, sometimes amounting to craving. Assuming this is correct, how does it arise?

The all-important first proposition is that this state of experience arises from unawareness of the nature of the human situation: from misconceptions concerning the nature of things; most briefly, from ignorance. From this beginning, the steps in the sequential pattern can be (and often are) numbered.

1. non-existence of insight or the absence of understanding is the root of dukkha.
   It gives rise to
2. a will to act,
   which gives rise to
3. a general conciousness,
   which gives rise to
4. the possibility of experiencing psycho-physical phenomena,
   which gives rise to
5. the six faculties, that is the five senses and the mind,
   which give rise to
6. contacts or activity of the six faculties
   which gives rise to
7. sensations, feelings, experience,
   which give rise to
8. desire, thirst, craving,
   which give rise to
9. the creation of attachment or bonds,
   which give rise to
10. the will to be, or the process of becoming,
    which gives rise to
11. birth in this world,
    which gives rise to

12. the ills that humans are heirs to: dissatisfaction, pain, suffering, and death.

Death is followed by re-incarnation and the cycle of rebirth is established: from this, attainment of nibbana provides the only escape.

This attempt at a quasi-logical pattern leading to the normal human state is a purely intellectual exercise with no support other than possible mental satisfaction.

In Buddhist thought, this scheme has at least two immediate influences. The reversal of these steps is one way of envisaging the attainment of nibbana, with its cessation of the rebirth of the individual. And these reverse stages are also related to the levels of experience in developed practices of Buddhist meditation. It could be suggested that having learnt this pattern, the disciple will be prepared to imagine, or to register, a succession of states corresponding to re-ascent of the ladder away from everyday existence.

The pattern of the Tathagata's teaching is claimed to be consistent with "the twelve links in the chain of causation". The sequence is initiated by ignorance and the over-coming of ignorance will lead to the destruction of the chain. The essential truth is that suffering is the necessary consequence of attachment to the things of this world, as it leads to the illusion of their ultimate significance.* The truth lies in the transcience of things. In this, and throughout the many forms taken by Buddhism, there is presented the Tathagata's insistence that the mind is the most significant aspect of the individual.

This conceptual scheme is known in Pali as *paticca-samuppada*, often translated as (the pattern of) "conditioned genesis". It implies that, for the individual, ultimate causation is of a mental character. I doubt whether any plausible justification for this hypothesis can be provided: certainly I know of none. Nevertheless, the assumed domination of mental causation has some consequences which, it could be argued, are at least pragmatically acceptable.

---

* It is from this point that much of Mahayana teaching departs widely from the Theravada. As will be explained later, several Mahayana schools deny the significance if not the reality of all experience in this world, i.e. they arrive at a version of solipsism.

mental states are all important. This is also a conclusion arrived at by many non-Buddhist philosophers and there is little need to elaborate on its wide approval. Each one of us is aware that as individuals, at any moment, the whole experience we have of the universe is carried in our minds. The most acute and "real" pain, say from a crushed foot, disappears when some part of the brain is influenced by drugs, or if our mind is dominated by a greater interest, such as escape from a violent pursuer. The professional philosopher would make this point far more carefully. All I am anxious to do is to insist that most of the time our experiences of ourselves and of our environment is a mental state.

This element in the Buddhist outlook is conducive to the development of detachment from what many would describe as the temptations of this world, and to the cultivation, by sustained practice, of relaxed mental states by meditative exercises.

It is no part of my presentation to argue that this "path of meditation" can be substantiated as effective for more than a minority of individuals. That many can achieve not only profound satisfaction but also a convicing depth of insight by meditation is beyond question. There are many others, of whom I am one, for whom this path seems closed. Undoubtedly, a sufficiently detemined degree of application could suffice to open the way for many. Those who have never learnt to swim, ski, or hang-glide are only distantly aware of the joys so to be attained: and those who have not successfully practised some detached meditation (yoga) remain in that unfulfilled state.

The cultivation of a widely extended pattern of meditation plays a major role in the life of the committed Buddhist disciple. It is accepted that meditation is important, both as a means of achieving a right understanding of the teaching of the Tathagata, and as a means of advancing towards nibbana. If, as many Theravadins would do, we substitute as an equivalent for *nibbana*, "the truth", then we can at least understand that this procedure comes close to that practised by the Christian mystics. And we can accept that it has been pursued by countless devotees to their experienced satisfaction. The quality and significance of "the truth" thus achieved would still have to be carefully examined.

Plate 1. Upper: Lumbini, the site of Gotama's birth. Now Rummindei in Nepalese Ṭerai.
Lower: Lumbini Pillar inscription announcing Asoka's visit and its result. See text page 138.

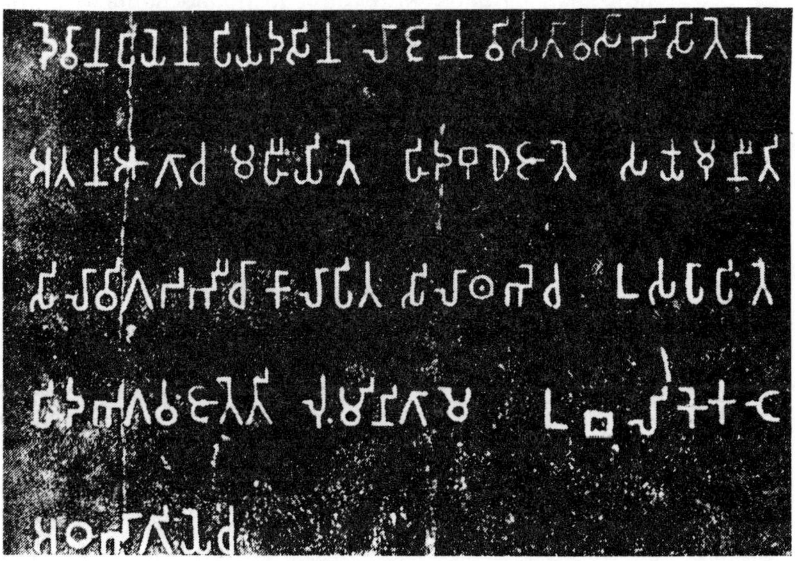

Plate 2. Upper: Bodh Gaya or Buddha Gaya, Bihar, India. Part of the bodhi tree and temple at the site where Gotama attained his enlightenment. The most venerated of all Buddhist sites. See text page 28.
Lower: The main stupa at Sanchi, India. In early tradition such mounds were built to house some supposed remains of Gotama.

Plate 3. Upper: The Asoka Lion column at Lauriya-Nandangarh, North India, 3rd century BC.
Lower: The lion captial of Asoka's column at Sarnath. 3rd century BC. Sarnath Museum. India's National Emblem is derived from this, with the three Lions mounted on the abacus carrying the wheel in the centre. i.e. The wheel of the Law, see text page 42. The base of the capital is an inverted lotus. Below the abacus the emblem has the words in Devanagari script: SATYAMEVA JAYATE, i.e. Truth alone triumphs. No symbol could be more completely Buddhist.

Plate 4. Two of the great number of Buddhist temples at Pagan on the Irrawaddy, Upper Burma; see text page 164. The upper photograph is the Ananda temple built in the 11th century AD. by Indian monks for King Kyanzittha. The lower is the 13th century Mingalazedi temple.

A more practical consequence to the emphasis on mental states is seen in the Buddhist view of "intention". This is regarded as all-important in making a moral or even legal judgement of a person's action. If it can be established that a crime was committed but with an almost complete absence of "intention", the perpetrator may go almost scot-free. A person proved to have the definite intention of murder, who only succeeds in disturbing or injuring this intended victim, such a person is only marginally different from a murderer. St. Paul also enunciated this view, and it is much favoured by psychologists. Without pursuing its evaluation, it can be said to correspond to much modern enlightened opinion.

There are dangers in the emphasis on mental causation. Ultimately it leads to solipsism — that we know only ourselves. There are notable schools of European philosophers who come close to this category. Whilst much has been written, from Berkeley onwards, in support of such views, they are largely intellectual exercises of a negative character. Most significant, in the present context, is the fact that a solopsist view is profoundly un-Buddhist. The whole aim of Gotama was to provide a path through life for other people, and his disciples were adjured to convey such enlightenment as they attained, to those others who enquired of it. The reality of other people was never in doubt.

More serious consequences follow from a tendency to accept that if all experience is in the mind, then solutions to the problems of this world can be achieved by meditation. It is with some reluctance that I suggest this attitude may be a major cause of the absence of recognizably scientific, or even of substantial empirical studies, in the classical Buddhist world. As far as I am aware, little progress, certainly no systematic developments, in science took place under the aegis of pure Buddhism. Many might think that an excellent restriction. But I would not be writing this in a comfortably heated room, with a stainless steel ball-point pen, and an ample supply of paper, if it were not for science. Neither would you, dear reader, have a printed copy of my comments to read. Needham, in his authoritative and extended account of science and civilization in China gives the largest element of stimulation to the Taoists. Buddhist influences were also involved but, most readers will accept the simple statement that science, as Europe has known it for three centuries, scarcely breathed in countries where Buddhism was widely received.

Earlier, I wrote "with some reluctance . . . this attitude may be a major cause" of the absence of scientific developments. It may be that I am mis-representing Buddhist attitudes: but I can only convey my own evaluation.

In considering the lack of Buddhist sponsorship of scientific studies what is probably even more significant than the emphasis on mental states, is the dominant concern of the Tathagata's teaching with the guidance of individuals past the trials of this world. Whilst Buddhism amply emphasizes the need for good works, for charity, for cooperation in eliminating undesirable social conditions, etc., such aims are mainly for the lay followers, and, in any case, are only secondary to the attainment of enlightenment. The "chain of conditioned causation" is entirely in terms of human experience and human action. Gotama was only concerned with matters of human conduct. (Confucius likewise).

It is an extreme, and an unjustified conclusion, that the pre-occupation with the individual's attainment of nibbana makes Buddhism merely a route for escape from this world. Gotama himself repeatedly recalled his own achievement of enlightenment, his conquest over the trials of this existence, and his own assurance of "no return" in any future re-birth. But he frequently insisted that that was not a sufficient end in itself. He had the obligation to convey his enlightenment to all who would be interested to learn of it. The same applies to all his disciples. Their own enlightenment must not be a selfish exercise: they must share their insights and help others along the path they are following. Despite all this, there was no incentive to provide an understanding of how the material and the living world had their observed characteristics. Here the never varying rule that members of the sangha (i.e. the Buddhist monks) needed only their saffron robes and their bowl for begging food, acted as a cut-off from any systematic concern with the behaviour of things. The structure of the natural world was not of concern to Buddhists: the Tathagata's concern was human behaviour.

In Europe many factors, undoubtedly including economic ones, eventually stimulated the rapid growth of science and technology. And there was available in the West the astonishing gift from the Greeks of logical and mathematical reasoning. A comment of Einstein's summarizes the situation. "the development of Western science has been based on two great achievements, the invention of the formal logical system (in Euclidean geometry) ... and the discovery of the possibility of finding out causal relationships by systematic experiment. ... One need not be astonished that the Chinese sages did not make these steps. The astonishing thing is that these discoveries were made at all."

In one important respect, the puzzlement over the lack of scientific developments in Buddhist countries is heightened by reference to the chain of "conditioned genesis (or formation)". The first element in this chain is the unawareness of the nature of things: lack of understanding: ignorance. It seems that "ignorance" here is perhaps less an absence of factual knowledge, than an inability to appreciate "the true nature of things". Even so, if acted on in the context of the world we live in, this elemental root to *dukka* would imply the need for an effort to pursue rational enquiries and so lead to science? That does not appear to have happened. However, it does mean that Buddhism is fully open to the aims of science in extending our knowledge of man and his world. The elements of honesty, truth, clarity, application, elimination of the supernatural, co-operation — and many other features characteristic of Buddhist thought — are all specifically favourable to science *per se*. A whole series of mostly desirable limitations appear as soon as the applications of science are considered in a Buddhist context. We shall return to this question, but, it will already be clear, that many of the major conceptual revolutions which science has achieved in the Judaeo-Christian-Moslem world, have always been acceptable in the Tathagata's enlightenment.

The immediately relevant specific feature of "conditioned genesis" is the first clause in the sequence. Lack of awareness and mistaken, misleading understanding is given as the root of *dukkha*. A lot can be said in nominating 'ignorance' as determinative in much of human distress. In my view, the "much" is not to be replaced by "all". So many of us, as individuals, pursue, with all vigour, ends which we feel are desirable, but which frequently prove illusory: that is, the pleasure of attainment bears little relation to the effort and sacrifice involved. This is so widespread an experience that genuine exceptions may be relatively few. The reader may well feel that a wet blanket is being prepared to smother all enthusiastic personal effort. That is not the case. What is suggested is that we should not fool ourselves by exaggerating the value of some possibly real satisfaction or by imagining others, which are either unworthy or do not, in truth, exist.

One, not too trivial example. In the post-1950 years college students have acquired a whole range of freedoms for which, on occasions, they have literally fought and screamed. From direct observation, they are in no way in as happy a state as their predecessors sixty years ago. In terms of satisfaction, they seem to have aimed at the wrong ends. We have all been young and made our mistakes: and it is not very helpful to suggest that the experience needed to minimize wrong choices usually comes only with age, unless it is accepted from one's elders.

The Buddhist thesis is that desires must be critically controlled as they so often lead to illusory, and, even more often, to transient satisfaction. Disappointment and disillusion are not experiences to be sought after: ignorance can be their source. The greater the craving, the greater can be the disillusion and eventual distress. The pattern is only too well known in terms of drugs.

In giving ignorance as a principal cause of failure and distress in human affairs, the Tathagata has some notable successors. Socrates, Plato and Spinoza are three who claimed that all wrong action is due to intellectual error. They believed that any person of mature understanding will choose and act wisely: by that they mean that individuals will pursue courses leading to minimum distress to themselves and to their communities. Spinoza's views can be stated concisely: ignorance is the source of all sin. This deviates from the Tathagata's thesis only in the sense that he would not use the word 'sin': in the Buddhist world there is nothing to sin against. Where, in this statement, Spinoza (for whom the whole world and everything in it was a manifestation of God) uses 'sin', Gotama would insert 'dukkha'.

Dr. Michael Carrithers in a careful presentation of Buddhist principles, based also on much study of practices, briefly expounds the role of ignorance or delusion:*

> "In the Buddha's usage, however, his knowledge was not so much an esoteric truth like the knowledge of the nature of the Self, but rather a penetrating understanding of *things as they are*. By comparison people are ordinarily not so much uninformed — as one might be uninformed of tax laws or of the nature of the Self — but positively deluded. They are mistaken, so, craving has its way with them. The relationship between craving, ignorance and suffering is rather like the relationship between heat, oxygen and fire. Heat (craving) is the motive force, but without oxygen (ignorance) fire (suffering) could not arise."

When one sees how the world, from the level of personal relations to that of intercontinental rivalries, is beset with confrontations and hostilities, it is in no way irrelevant to suggest that ignorance is a major root of conflict. One of the functions of academic history is to explain how past conflicts arose because of contradictory views. Often those views were not only equally cogent but also equally reasonable to each of the two opposing sides, but generally ill-understood by the other. The American Revolution and War of Independence is a prime instance. It can be written down as a result of ignorance, if not of wilful misunderstanding by both sides. (This is not to say that the consequences were ill: that judgement can rarely be made, as history is irreversible.) In a basic sense, the Tathagata here stands acompanied by Confucius and even by Plato: each insists that enlightenment is a prime requisite in the guidance of a nation.

It is one aspect of the tragic human situation that the leaders of groups will only rarely be balanced individuals. To see the alternative sides to questions is no way to acquire a controlling role in affairs. But it can be claimed for Buddhism that, more than any other philosophy, it has a clearer basis for elevating lack of understanding as a major contributor to human difficulties. It enunciates this as the first element in the chain of "conditioned beginnings".

* Michael Carrithers, *The Buddha*, Oxford University Press. (Past Masters paperback) 1983.

It must be emphasized that no good Buddhist, that is, one fully conscious of and committed to the teaching of the Tathagata, would make any such claim, or any comparison with other teachings. Not only should modesty preclude any possible mention of superiority: it is unacceptable to point out weaknesses in the beliefs of others until they find themselves in difficulties and ask for help. The truth will, in any case, prevail. The Tathagata had found the truth.

The middle way and toleration

The Theravada Buddhist is constantly aware of the problems and perils facing the individual in this life. Whilst fully alerted to the consequences of an ill-informed choice, he is nevertheless, as a layman, not to abandon an active life in the world. Even if it were only symbolically inserted in all the accounts of the Tathagata's life, it is of the greatest significance that he categorically rejected the role of an ascetic. Between self-denial and self-indulgence, the middle way is the path of reason.

Although Buddhist schools have developed extensive metaphysical systems and much philosophic discussion, these stand in the form of intellectual backcloths to the pattern of behaviour encapsulated in the eight-fold path. The temptation to produce a definitive holy writ has been resisted by almost all the many schools. Buddhism has no accepted gospel statement. There are many expressions in a codified, or at least enumerated form, of the rules of behaviour: but there is nothing remotely equivalent to the Athanasian creed or the thirty-nine articles of the Anglican church. The avoidance of bitter controversies which this absence of dogmatic statement has achieved is remarkable. It stems from the open-mindedness of the Tathagata, and his insistence that, with the general guidelines he proferred, there was no course possible other than for each individual to seek his (or her) own enlightenment.

Through the centuries the Tathagata and his followers have been primarily concerned with those who sought their teaching. In the absence of dogmatic beliefs, they have never been anxious to challenge other sects, or even individuals, to justify their positions. This has made the Buddhists amongst the most tolerant of all committed, organized groups. Combined with their adherence to non-violence, it might well have led to their suppression by more aggressive elements. This certainly happened in India with the Moslem invasion of the twelfth century. But generally, Buddhist communities have survived even in the harshest environments, and at least in part, because they offered no positive threat to non-Buddhists.

Tolerance in matters of other people's religion has historically been extended to great lengths in Buddhist circles. Unless they were violent or cruel they have invariably treated the practices of others with respect. In countries new to Buddhism, traditional beliefs have been generously assessed if they could in some way be described as leading, even if only primitively, to the individuals's approach to enlightenment. This permissiveness repeatedly led to the Tathagata's doctrine of self-discipline being much diluted, if not submerged, by mixture with other creeds. This will become clear later, in the references to non-Theravada Buddhism, and to Buddhism in Burma and Sri Lanka.

A significant aspect of Buddhist tolerance is seen in relation to the caste system. On joining the Buddhist community all caste or class status is, in principle, completely obliterated. The earliest accounts give instances of individuals of the most varied origin, from the highest to the lowest, being accepted into the monastic order. Nevertheless, there is no record of Buddhism acting to eliminate, or even advocating the abandonment of the caste system. It was, it seems, just ignored. Tolerance had dispelled any proselytizing fervour? Many might suggest that the neutral attitude, which seems to have been established by the Tathagata himself, arose from the fact that Gotama was born into the warrior caste and perhaps accepted the divisions as "natural". Furthermore, in India, Buddhism was always surrounded by the sea of Hinduism: to have challenged it in its most dogmatic aspect could have produced an unusually sharp antagonism, which could have not only hurt but must have led to the suppression of the Buddhist community. It is, of course, speculation that such calculated discretion was an element in the Buddhist behaviour.

Toleration has meant that religious wars are almost unknown in the Buddhist world. Wars have occurred between Buddhist peoples, but only infrequently and without great violence. So complete is the acceptance of *metta* (loving kindness) that such occasions have been rare.

One historically important instance of Buddhist conflict occurred in Burma in the eleventh century. In the north, there was established what appears to have been a version of Buddhism much degraded by mixture with the Hinduism of neighbouring Indian provinces. The northern king at Pagan, Anawrahta, learnt of the much purer Theravada Buddhism to be found in the south. Accordingly, he made that region the object of his conquest: after which he returned, taking with him relics, accounts of the teaching, and well-instructed Theravada scholars. With these, he instituted a notable period of purified Buddhism whose advancement became one of the principal aims of his dynasty. Successive kings vied with one another in temple construction. Their efforts now provide the extensive and truly impressive remains to be seen along five miles of the Irrawaddy. This site of the large city of Pagan was devastated by the forces of Kublai Khan in 1287.

More than a thousand years before Anawrahta at Pagan, the greatest of Indian emperors, Asoka (269–232 B.C.), had become a Buddhist and showed his concern for its advancement by erecting inscriptions in stone expounding its teachings. The inscription on one of his famous pillars carries (it can be read today) a commendation of tolerance: "His sacred and gracious majesty the king does reverence to men of all sects, whether ascetics or laymen, by gifts and other forms of respect. His majesty, however, cares not so much for gifts and the show of reverence as that there should be a growth of the essentials of the matter in all sects . . . the root of it is restraint of speech so that a man must not do reverence to his own religion or disparage that of others without reason. He who would do so in reality then inflicts injury on his own sect. Concord is to be praised and so also listening willingly to the piety accepted by other people. This is the desire of his majesty." Twenty-two hundred years later, this message could well be engraved throughout Northern Ireland.

One aspect of the composure allied to tolerance is the open-minded attitude towards non-Buddhists. By the same token, no individual is regarded as beyond the possibility of enlightenment. Vicious characters have been restrained and punished: if they show no interest in improving their ways, it is confidently expected that kamma will lead to their eventual bad end. Evil is to be avoided by following the middle way.

As numerous representations of the Tathagata imply, compassion is one of the supreme virtues of the Buddhist world. Growth in discipleship is reflected by the extension of compassion beyond one's own neighbours until it embraces the world and all that live in it. Whilst the question can be raised as to how frequently such a level of benevolence is achieved, the relevant message is that this has been the ideal in Buddhism from its foundation. The followers of Gotama did not have to wait until the twentieth century to preach the thesis of one world. They have never recognized barriers between races, classes, or creeds. The individual on the eight-fold path is expected no more to harm others than he would injure himself, and he must see the need and the means to remove impediments which restrict his magnanimity towards others.

The emphasis on self-discipline and self-effort towards enlightenment results in great significance being attached to each individual appreciating the nature of the self. As will appear later, Gotama was one of the earliest, if not the first philosopher to clarify the illusion of an identifiable stable self. He explained that what we so often regard as a constant element, that is one's own self, is an illusion, built on a succession of continually varying states. The Tathagata claims that that realization provides the basis for the expansion of the mistakenly narrow, confined view of the self. Our nature is such that we are, each of us, participating in a larger experience. Be that as it may, the Tathagata avers that as our insight increases, the more we become aware of the extension of our experience and sympathies far beyond the boundaries of the conventional self. Cultivating an identification with others sharing this life, the good Buddhist aims to realize that the whole world and all individuals are intimately and indissolubly linked.

Again, whilst this may represent an advanced stage of enlightenment, the character and direction of the Buddhist ideal is clear.

The eight-fold path provides a pattern leading to the highest standards of behaviour. Its full detail is intended for the monks, or those who are totally committed to attaining nibbana. The layman is encouraged along the same way. There is no concept of sin in Buddhism. No one is irretrievably damned, and in the Theravada school, there is no consignment to the torture chambers of hell. However, there are the strongest prohibitions. No one should (i) harm life: (ii) take what is not offered: (iii) indulge in extra marital sex or lewd behaviour: (iv) tell untruths or indulge in harmful talk: (v) partake of alcoholic drinks or use drugs.

In the family, each member must respect and help the others and such kindnesses as are natural there should be extended to all one's friends and associates. Generosity is much to be encouraged, but must never lead to ostentation. Charitable works, service to the community, consideration for others in all its forms, are obvious virtues. 'He who attends to the sick attends to me'', was Gotama's expression of approval for care of the suffering. As there is no concept of sin, so is there no concept of reward for right action. To the Buddhist, benevolence is its own reward: it should be practised spontaneously without any conscious or unconscious thought of "doing good". Progress along the eight-fold path eventually leads to a state of moral purity "beyond good and evil".

The precepts sketched here are shared by many other philosophies and religions. In Buddhism they are clearly spelt out in the earliest records. Amongst the very numerous sects that have arisen from the Tathagata's original teaching, there are notable variations of emphasis and even, in some, notable departures from the original clear guidance. Nevertheless, the uniformity in the major aspects of the moral code has been impressively constant through the centuries.

The middle-way and toleration in Buddhism contribute to the equanimity which markedly characterized the Tathagata. There are many instances of this in the Theravada canon.

On one occasion Gotama and his followers come across an ascetic heaping abuse on the Buddha, who is being defended by a disciple. The latter's efforts only drew more excessive slanders from the wild man. Gotama's comment was:

"If anyone were to find fault with me or the doctrine or the order (of monks), do not be offended or ruffled. If for any reason you become perturbed, it will be to your own disadvantage. Rather, when people hurl abuse and criticize you, you should stop to think whether there is any truth in what they say or whether it is quite false. Likewise, when praise is expressed, you should not necessarily pay any attention: rather, consider it calmly."

Not surprisingly, the Tathagata was frequently challenged by adversaries to defend his teaching. One such occasion was the encounter with General Siha, a prominent Jain disciple. He charged Gotama with being a retailer of pessimism and a fatalistic believer in inaction. "Well," came the reply, "I could be described as an inactivist as I do press on my disciples to be inactive with respect to many aspects of undesirable conduct. But equally you could call me an activist in that I advocate positive effort towards good conduct, self-discipline, and consideration for others."

Gotama proceeded to expound the essentials of his teaching, as it constantly recurs in the accounts of his activities. And, as on many other occasions, the record claims that General Siha was so impressed by the presentation that he asked to be accepted as a disciple. This is not immediately granted, as Gotama points out he is a well-known public figure, and such persons must not be seen to act rashly or to change allegiance readily. However, having seen the light, the General is not prepared to contemplate leaving it, and he is accordingly accepted as a disciple of the Buddha — but on condition that he continues to support the Jains with whom he had previously been associated.

The Jains most notable characteristic was their unqualified acceptance of *ahimsa* — respect for life in all its forms. Their great teacher, known to us as Mahavira, was a contemporary of Gotama's, and there are many accounts of Jain disciples approaching the Tathagata and questioning him. Several of these encounters proceed and end as did General Siha's.

Then there is the Tathagata's visit to the Kalamas. These people were regarded as sharply intelligent: they certainly wished to question Gotama on the validity of the several doctrines which were currently being offered them. The advice took the form: "Do not accept a teaching because it has been traditionally supported for however long: nor from its description as sacred: not from its apparently logical appeal or plausibility: not because it appears convenient to your wishes: not out of respect for the teacher. But when you know for yourselves that certain things are unprofitable, unworthy, untrue, and damaging, then surely you should reject them." There follows a statement of Gotama's analysis of the "the ills of the world" and of his middle way.

It is the rejection of any dogmatic approach and the appeal to each individual's assessment of his experience which is so enlightening. There is no attempt to issue an *ex-cathedra* statement: nor is there any attempt to claim any special status by the Tathagata. He was clearly so confident that he had, at least, a good approximation to the truth: and that the truth would prevail.

This exchange with the Kalamas has a special appeal. The account has the quality of the direct report of a historical occurrence. It gives the Tathagata the urbane, open-minded character so generally claimed for him. And it amounts to an extended, explicit insistence on determinative empiricism. Few statements could be closer to the practice of the investigating scientist.

In this approach, the appeal of the Tathagata's outlook is universal. It is not only immediately acceptable to all thinking men and women, regardless of their origin, but it is equally valid "yesterday, today, and for future times". Whatever one concludes on the adequacy of Gotama's teaching, his modest confidence, open approach, deep concern, and profound compassion mark him as one of the greatest of the sons of women.

Nibbana

Much in Buddhist teaching, and in the instruction of the monks, is concerned with the various stages through which those who have accepted the Tathagata as a teacher must pass in order to achieve their ultimate freedom from longing. An elaborate training in meditation is one of the features of such progress. The novice starts on these stages — so said Gotama — when he has grasped the significance of dukkha — that the ills of the world result from selfish desires. Nibbana is the final stage on this path of enlightenment, it is the ultimate goal traditional to Buddhism.

Nibbana (Sanskrit: nirvana) is repeatedly characterized as beyond description in words: which immediately suggests it may be in the realm of mysticism. However, the Theravada canon offers many expressions by the Tathagata which approach a definition:

The cessation of becoming.

The elimination of desire, of hatred, of illusion.

The extinction of (all that is meant by) thirst.

The real, the excellent, the calming of all desires, the elimination of dukkha.

Freed from ignorance, of the cycle of rebirths, of all discontent and longing: beyond tracing. Completely extinguished (as a lamp is extinguished).

Unconditioned by this world's restraints.

Although frequently described in negative terms, nibbana is definitely not annihilation of the 'self', as Buddhism denies, with impressively cogent clarity, the existence of any permanent 'self'. Perhaps an acceptable approximation is to say that nibbana is freedom from all evil, craving, hatred, and ignorance. In this sense it can be accepted as a meaningful, if demanding, ideal for the twentieth century Buddhist. It is not a state to be achieved in some other world. An essential part of the age-long appeal of the Buddha lies in his insistence that this ideal can be reached in this world.* If, for most of us, this is unduly optimistic, at least it disposes of the view that Buddhism is a pessimistic philosophy.

Coomaraswamy offers an enlightening comment. 'Nibbana', this brahmin scholar explains, literally means "dying out" or "extinction", as of a fire. It is used by the Tathagata in this general sense. In the Upanishads (and, therefore, in Hinduism) it means perfect self-realization: there, those in whom the darkness of ignorance and limited understanding has been overcome by complete enlightenment are those faced with the ultimate experience of nibbana. The Buddhist use of nibbana emphasizes the "dying out" aspect, not the dying out of a soul or of individuality, but rather the release from all thirst, resentment, and delusion.

A helpful lay comment, which is probably far from what traditional Buddhist scholars would accept, offers a realistic approach. "The Budda himself assures us we can all attain nibbana, but realistically it seems altogether too grandly

* Buddhist scholars make a distinction between nibbana which is to be achieved, usually after many rebirths, in this world, and parinibbana which is attained when a fully enlightened one finally leaves this world.

remote for us to attain. As a result, we feel discouraged, and wonder whether Buddhism really has anything to offer us? It is vital to realize that enlightenment is not an 'all or nothing' ideal, but something which grows day by day. We do not remain totally lost and unenlightened until, one far distant day, there comes a magical moment when, 'ping', we suddenly enter nibbana. Rather, by following the Buddhist way of life, we become more enlightened from one week to the next."

Although much diluted by comparison with Theravada teaching, this seems a very reasonable appraisal. It is important to remember that the Tathagata is not going to rescue us from the human predicament, but an acceptance of his guidance can lead to what is described in Buddhism as enlightenment.

It seems to me that one can accept the significance and the essential validity of the teaching of Gotama without being saddled with the concept of nibbana with its traditional content and its consequences. In any case, there is much to be considered in relation to nibbana as a key element in the customary presentation of Buddhism.

The extended illustrations of nibbana in negative terms convey an experiece of triumph over the pitfalls and delusions of existence. The fact that such accounts convey little or nothing which can be grasped does not disturb the Theravadins, who tend to reply: nibbana is not to be grasped, it is to be experienced. Experience of the indescribable makes no great appeal to reason, although we must remember that Mozart, Beethoven and Schubert (amongst others) have been well characterized as expressing the inexpressible.

By its nature, nibbana is at the limit of the esoteric. No evidence of its reality exists for the outsider. In that respect it has the same fictitious character as the traditional Christian heaven. No one knows where it is, nor of anyone having got there. In both communities, immense numbers would say they believed in this state: and, in both communities, it makes little difference that the state is a mental creation. The members are equally motivated by the prospect of a state which exists only in anticipation. This, perhaps, is a little hard on the Buddhists, who would claim that nibbana can be attained in this life. What is lacking, in their case, is any shred of evidence that the attainment contributes anything to one of their essential aims, that is, to the elimination of the cycle of rebirth.

A discussion of the rebirth thesis is difficult. No significant evidence for it appears to be available: relevant, in a general sense, to this conclusion is a consideration of immortality, of which there is a later mention. With the rejection of the idea of rebirth, and the previous qualification of the significance of nibbana, many emphases in the historic doctrine of Buddhism are lost.

The account already given of the strands in the eight-fold path follows the traditional presentation. In those features, the ultimate motivation is the achievement of nibbana. None of them can be in any way less worthy of pursuit even if nibbana be a fiction, but some of the emphasis, or at least some of the procedures, in the cultivation of right mindfulness, concentration, and thought, might be seen as less demanding if there is no rebirth to be escaped. But the loss may be merely in relation to what has been historically regarded as the goal. The whole pattern, nevertheless, retains its inherent value. In no way are the eight strands of smaller human value in conducing to a state of fully alerted, calm insight, a deep appreciation of things as they are, and an understanding (in terms propounded by the Tathagata) of how the trials of this world may be faced.

The canonical texts and almost all later expositions direct the individual along the eight-fold path as the means of avoiding rebirth, itself regarded as a further subjection to trial and tribulation. In the absence of nibbana, the individual will be aiming at enlightenment for its own sake — the clear understanding of the character of human existence and of the forces which shape it.

Few philosophies, and no religions, argue the case for the good life being its own reward. The religions always offer a large imaginary carrot, usually to be arrived at "in the next world". Buddhism has traditionally offered nibbana, perhaps only less hypothetical than heaven in that it was potentially attainable in this world. Certainly, as a carrot, nibbana was a rather dim offer. No sense of achievement or of satisfaction was involved: it was a fade-out of all feelings and thought. The nibbana-sceptic may surely argue that the moral goals in Buddhism should be accepted for their own sakes.

In the western world, nibbana and the cycle of rebirths,

cannot have much credibility. Those humanists who have expressed their deep appreciation of Gotama's teaching must have accepted it as being its own reward. At the end of twentieth century, it does not seem that such a detached appraisal and acceptance will become widespread. Many more generations, rejecting the heavens and other fictions of the past, will be needed before the further maturity inherent in rational Buddhism becomes generally acceptable.

Another important change follows the rejection of nibbana as a specific, defined, goal. It should follow that the individual would be less concerned with the withdrawal from this world, progress in which isolationist direction measures the approach to nibbana. It has been the historic criticism of the Theravada school that its concern has been too much restricted to the individual. In a large degree, this is the very aspect which led to the creation of the Mahayana school, whose emphasis was on taking Buddhism to all the people. There is only the least of doubts, however, that the Theravadins were, in this respect at least, following Gotama's emphasis.

The sangha, the community of the monks, was one of the three jewels of Buddhism. Only by withdrawing from the distractions of home life and the market place was there practical possibility for individuals to achieve the detachment necessary in progress to nibbana. As the Buddha realized, after his own enlightenment, this was certain to be too difficult a proposition for most people: even so, the Pali canon mentions lay persons who achieved full enlightenment.

It must never be forgotten that the concepts of re-birth and nibbana were firmly established in the Vedic world of Gotama's time. Even when extolling the virtues of the Tathagata, many commentators, especially those closer to or actually within the ambit of Hinduism, point out that he was seen as a revolutionary in doctrine by his contemporaries. He made it clear that he was convinced of the falseness of animism on the one hand, and of the dogmatic supernaturalism of the Brahmins on the other. It has been suggested that he might well have made a decisive break from the traditional beliefs in the cycle of rebirth and in nibbana were the community pressures in their favour not so intense. This is to suggest that the Tathagata compromised in his stance, accepting items which he might have refuted in order to avoid an overwhelming rejection of his teaching by his contemporaries. Whilst this cannot be proved, there would appear to be indications in its favour.

Accepting that nibbana was an essential feature in the religio-philosophical thought of Gotama's contemporaries (as was 'heaven' for all Christians in, say, the sixteenth century), then, whilst he used the term, he certainly changed its meaning. How far he moved from the Hindu usage connoting union of the individual with the Universal Being (whatever that might be), is seen in his frequent identification of nibbana with the truth. The strength of this view is registered by his own preference for the title Tathagata, which is interpreted as 'one who has arrived (at the truth)'. Even if, as Lessing poetically emphasized, we cannot arrive at the truth, it is a far more meaningful concept than most glosses of nibbana.

The dominant influence of Hinduism is most clearly seen in the changes undergone by the Buddhist schools from *ca* 300 B.C. forwards. Already by Asoka's time (250 B.C.), significant groups had come forward with an altogether far wider, quite unhistoric presentation of Buddhism. These sects promoted the inclusion of a multiplicity of newly imagined buddhas and bodhisattvas as a means of providing a more colourful, stimulating, and acceptable version of Gotama's teaching for the layperson. These elements matched the polytheistic imagery of Hindus. A brief account of this, the Mahayana school of Buddhism, will come later. Here, suffice it to say that it embodies degrees of irrationality and meaninglessness which are beyond my description. Much of it is in aid of the thesis that everything is nothing, all is void. There is a clear intention to defy sense and to indulge in a free-ranging exercise of heated imagination. This gives rise not so much to accounts of the indescribable as to reports of the inconceivable.

Returning to the status of the nibbana concept. Walpola Rahula (loc.cit. footnote, p.36) offers a significant comment. "It is interesting to note that this definition of *nirodha* (cessation of dukkha) which is found in the first sermon of the Buddha at Sarnath, does not contain the word *nibbana,* though the definition means it." In another commentary, a no less competent a scholar, Susumu Yuamaguchi, Professor of Buddhist studies at Kyoto University, states that the question whether rebirth was accepted as inevitable in early Buddhism has always been, and is still being, debated. Accordingly, we shall not perhaps be isolated, nor even in bad company within the Buddhist community (although neither of these criteria should determine one's position), if we reject the idea of rebirth and insist on a non-mystical interpretation of nibbana.

Two further aspects of Buddhist thought provide encouragement for such reassessments. The first is the explicit denial of absolutes. Comments on the major significance of this denial have already been made. The second is the Tathagata's constantly repeated admonition that each one of us must find his/her own enlightenment: that we should accept nothing, even of his own teaching, of which we are not convinced: that we must "come and see". And so we are free to assess the teaching which comes in his name to the best of our own critical ability.

The self

Remembering that Gotama expounded his philosophy even some centuries before the greatest of the Greeks, one of his most extraordinary insights is provided by his analysis of the immediate, abiding concept which dominates our waking thoughts: the self, the I, the ego of which we are all aware.

Basic to Buddhist thought is the claim that nothing of which we have experience is permanent. This, of course, was also the conclusion of one of Gotama's contemporaries. Heraclitus enunciated '*panta rhei*': everything flows. The same thesis plays a recurrent role in Buddhism. The operation of kamma and the "conditioned origination" with its cycle of stages, developing from lack of knowledge or uncertainty, has already been sketched. This wheel of change is constantly invoked. Gotama's first response when faced by a human problem was to seek its immediate cause, and then to trace a sequence of steps which, in his view, had led and would continue to lead to a similar state of affairs.

Each life is a dynamic process. No-one remains constantly the same. What we identify as "I" is likewise in flux. There is no separate ego above or beyond the kaleidoscope of impressions which each individual normally experiences. Insofar as there is uninterrupted change, some elements contributing to the impression of self disappear and are replaced by new elements arising from our experience in time.

Although we each usually cling with a profound concern to the identity of "I", only a little consideration is needed to realize it is not unchanging. There is an obvious practical sense in which one's ego is maintained. Between birth and death there is a continuity of experiences within the one person. And there are schools of thought which would insist that there is constancy in, what they might call, the "real self". Buddhism denies the existence of such a "real self".

The "self" we are now considering is that of which we are conscious, and it can perhaps be identified with our self-awareness, or our self-awareness plus the memories which each individual carries. It is the physical continuity of one's body and our mentally formulated memories which lead to the mistaken assumption of an invariant "I". However, the physical body can be seen to change: and, more important than the visible changes, are those in the physical system such as general health, nervous responses, and, perhaps most significant, the levels of glandular activity. The material composition of our bodies no less than the content of our minds is in constant flux. Also, our memories are subject to change. That we ascribe a permanent identity to ourselves and to other individuals is a convention and a pragmatic convenience: the permanence does not survive a calm analysis.

Gotama in discussing the changing nature of the self frequently had recourse to an analogy. Whilst analogies never prove anything, they possibly illustrate a valid resemblance. Gotama's instance was the sequence of changes in one material: milk turns to curds, which become butter, and then ghee (clarified butter). The sequence is a regular gradual progression: it is difficult to draw a sharp line where one changes to another: no new material is necessarily added: and yet the stages are recognizably different. The same happens to the personality. In many individuals marked changes are obvious, especially say, with illness or after medical treatment. No-one is asked to abandon the convincing experience of "myself". What is asked is the intellectual acceptance that the self is not constant, defined or abiding. It is thc supposed constancy which leads to the belief that there is within one an entity which might even persist after death.

Carrithers quotes a Theravada text: "What is called

'mentality' and 'mind' and 'consciousness' arises and ceases, in one way and another, through the day and night, just as a monkey ranging through a forest seizes a branch and, letting go, seizes another.' The illusion of constancy is the trap into which we fall: it is as unnatural and as frustrating, according to another Theravada text "as a dog tied to a post".

All this may be rather obvious, although not yet universally accepted. We are considering it only because Gotama was explicit on this question. He used his dismissal of the permanent self to expose numerous instances of distress, and in particular mental anxiety, as being the consequence of a mistaken belief in a constant "I".

This self-conciousness which is a major element in the self, is to be differentiated from the soul, which is also assumed to exist by so many people. Whilst everyone (with very few exceptions) is invariably experiencing an awareness of self, whose non-permanence and ultimate unreality is being considered here, the soul (at least in the religious and most philosophical systems) is another, different, concept. The experience of the self is, surely, of an entity subject to changes and, specifically, ranges of mood. Some selfs are notably equi-tempered: others (and it is part of the "identity" of the individual) show a wide range of emotional response. The soul (as I understand it) is not liable to be influenced by alcohol.

It may be of interest to offer a very brief summary of the Buddhist analysis of the human experience into five categories or aggregates. If the Pali records are to be believed, there is no doubt that this analysis was given first by Gotama himself. The five aggregates are:

(i) the aggregate of physical experience, i.e., material systems and their changes. It is of historical interest that the material elements are named as air, earth, fire and water (as in Aristotle): and the principal qualities as solidity, fluidity, heat, and motion.

(ii) the aggregate of sensations or feelings, whose origin is in the sense organs: the eye, the nose, the ear, the tongue, the body (touch) and the mind. The inclusion of the mind as a "sense organ" is of great interest. We need only say that mind is clearly described by the Tathagata as the organ responsible for appreciating mental conceptions, thoughts, and opinions. As the eye receives shapes and colours, the ear sounds, so does the mind receive ideas. Whatever else may be concluded on this simple characterization of mind, it clearly shows the originality, and some would say the depth, of the Tathagata's thought. We may, also, recall the important stress he gives (e.g., in the eight-fold path) to the proper use and discipline of all six faculties.

(iii) the process of learning by forming ideas and connecting mental impressions: the practice of imagination.

(iv) the aggregate of acts of willing, the making of conscious decisions and intentions. This aggregate is of importance as upon it depends (in Buddhist thought) the kamma effects to which the individual will be liable.

(v) the aggregate of consciousness. This "aggregate" forms a necessary addendum, as the Buddhist is taught to be specifically conscious of the signals he is receiving from the six senses. This is another instance of the emphasis on mental processes: the Buddhist is to be aware of the quality of the vision, the character of the scene and the changes in it, etc., as he looks out on the world. And the same for the other senses. In this way he cultivates and controls a heightened level of conscious awareness.

It is on the basis of these five aspects of the totality of experience that Gotama rejected the concept of a permanent self. This five-part description is intended to make clear the ever changing basis of what we experience as "I".

There are other consequences of this patten. Our conscious experience is the result of these several components and cannot be conceived as existing without them. Accordinly, in the Buddhist world there is no possible meaning to any form of "spirit" existence. The material body and the senses based on the eye, etc., are essential requirements before consciousness arises. It is extraordinary to find this clearly expounded twenty-five hundred years ago. In the West we are still plagued with endless varieties of spiritualism and we even have musically inclined mediums writing down what Mozart has recently composed in some other world. The negation of this fiction is provided by the message itself.

The emphasis on the impermanence of "the self" is a profound element in Buddhism. The transitory nature of existence is, of course, expounded in most religions and philosophies, but the Buddhist rarely allows it out of his mind.

It becomes part of the detachment which he seeks from this world. Other philosophies or religions have a belief in "the soul" or some related concept of a permanent element of the self. Not so the Buddhist, for whom the final change of death is all part of the sequence of events from birth. As the dissatisfaction and distress, which is dukkha, so largely arises from the impermanence of things, the Buddhist outlook is closely knit to reality. One comes back to the thesis that dissatisfaction often arises from the failure to realize the impermanence of things, that is, from ignorance. Overcoming ignorance eliminates dissatisfaction, and the individual moves forward on the path of enlightenment.

The detail and quality of Gotama's analysis of the self was almost certainly stimulated by prevailing Brahminical teaching with which he would have been familiar. In that philosophy there is an element of self-identification of the individual with the universe. Its aim is to experience the all-embracing Self and to merge one's identity with it. One must accept that there are many who can not only make sense of this, but who also find it deeply satisfying.

There are (certainly for me) uncertainties in what is meant by some details in the Tathagata's analysis of the self, but there is no doubt about its general conclusions. It is appropriate to quote some part of what David Hume (1711–76), one of the greatest of European philosophers, wrote on this question.

> 'For my part, when I enter most intimately into what I call *myself*, I always stumble on some particular perception or other, of heat or cold, light or shade, love or hatred, pain or pleasure. I never catch *myself* at any time without a perception, and *never can observe anything but the perception.*"
>
> (M.D.: his emphasis).

After commenting on the fact that many philosophers seem able to identify a well-defined self, he proceeds:

> "but setting aside some metaphysicians of this kind, I may venture to affirm of the rest of mankind, that they are nothing but a bundle or collection of different perceptions, which succeed each other with inconceivable rapidity, and are in a perpetual flux and movement."

As was Hume's genius, his thoughts are conveyed so

brilliantly clearly and concisely. Especially in the latter respect, he is far ahead of Siddhattha Gotama; but the agreement in their assessments could scarcely be closer. The same agreement can also be averred with Russell's analysis of the individual (see especially p.319 in his *Human Knowledge*, 1948) although I gathered Russell was not too anxious to emphasize any congruence, in this particular respect, with Buddha.

The Christian Soul, the Buddhist No-Soul, and Immortality

The Theravada sources of Buddhism make clear the Tathagata's view that the self is, at best, a convenient fiction and of significance only at a conventional level of day-to-day identity. Equally clearly, the same sources dismiss the existence of the soul. That this is a different matter is obvious when one remembers that the self, when regarded as real, has no necessary existence beyond the limits of birth and death of the individual: whilst the soul can, and often has been, envisaged as existing before birth and, almost invariably, is said to persist after death. In fact it is usually invoked in order to ensure that some part or trace of the individual will survive death.

There may well be readers who would not wish to differentiate between the self and the soul, but they will accept that most people do make such a distinction. As the Buddhist position is to deny the meaningful existence of both, consideration of the special character of the soul is necessary.

There are two points I would wish the reader to accept. Firstly, in this discussion I shall be comparing the Buddhist and the Christian views on subjects of some importance, and on which they differ. It cannot be too strongly emphasized that this is a very un-Buddhist procedure. The Tathagata most explicitly told his disciples never to make unfavourable remarks on other doctrines which people held in respect or in faith. He regarded all religions as an attempt, however mistaken in some cases, to come to terms with human existence. His particular wish was that all would, eventually, seek the enlightenment he claimed to dispense. Accordingly, he would have disapproved of the presentation I shall give.

C. A. F. Rhys Davids, one of the great European scholars of Buddhism, suggested that its philosophy can be summarized:

sabbam amiccam, sabbam dukkham, all is impermanent, all is liable to suffering. In no constituent of the living being was any exception to this rule of nature to be found. And since *atta* (the soul) as currently taught (in the Indian world), was essentially permanent, unchanging, blissful, powerful, there could be none of *atta* so conceived in the living being." This view Davids supported by quotations from the early records of Gotama's discourses. And he makes a significant further comment. "The individual is entirely phenomenal, governed by the laws of life. Were there in him a microcosmic emanation of the superphenomenal, he would have the power of deity to remould himself 'nearer to the heart's desire', and thus at will to transcend those laws."

The soul looms large in Christian belief: at least my understanding is that this has always been so, especially, and obviously so, in those eras during which the Christian Church had a dominant role in European culture. Perhaps the devil may quote, not scripture, but St. Augustine. The Christian religion "constitutes the simple way for the salvation of souls, for souls can be saved by no other way but this . . . And outside the church no one receives or retains final salvation." And to the Christian, Christianity embodies the eternal verities: so the soul must still be important. My second point of explanation is that my own assessment of what I have found from accounts of the Christian soul is the reverse of convincing. I hope I can assume that what I write will not pain anyone.

It might be asked: why draw in the Christian soul in a discussion of Buddhism? There are two reasons. As the Buddhist does not recognize its existence, one must go to another source to find what significance and value this concept possesses. And as most readers, even if not strictly Christians, will be aware of the importance of the soul in that religion, it provides a basis for meaningful discussion. One must, in fact, start from the Christian soul. Perhaps the reader will be patient in following my search for it.

Having only some bare acquaintance with the elements of eschatology and related topics, I was obliged to refer to what might be regarded as standard reference works.

In the *Hastings Encyclopaedia of Religion* there is an essay of great erudition by H. Wheeler Robinson. Whilst a pleasure to read as an article of scholarship, it is sadly weak in providing some indication of the existence of the item it so learnedly discusses. (How, many readers will ask, could it then be scholarly? I am obliged to reply that much scholarship is devoted to the ill-defined and, on occasions, to the non-existent.) The nearest it comes is as follows: "The soul is, in this article, taken in its most comprehensive sense, as denoting the whole 'self' or personality, the essential principle of human nature the basis of conscious, continuous, individual existence." Later, there is a further statement: "The term 'soul' must be taken to mean, not the unknown substratum of certain phenomena, but the spiritual entity which *is* in its distinctive activities and qualities. Such are its possession of a unique individuality, of the freedom of real initiative, of non-material content." There are many who will find these statements adequate. I am not amongst them. The author makes no attempt even to suggest the evidence for the existence of the 'soul'.

The Catholic Commentary on Holy Scripture (1953: carrying the imprimatur) made many things clear. Firstly, that several different Hebrew and, thence, Greek terms were all, on occasion, translated as "soul", whose root meaning was close to "breath of life";* that the Bible disposes of any question of the pre-existence of the soul; that man is immortal; the body and soul being reunited in the resurrection. "It is due to man's spiritual soul that his mental powers differ essentially from those of even the highest of the brute creation." The supreme aim of Christian practice is the soul's salvation.

St. Thomas Aquinas was explicit in his views: God cannot create men without souls, and each soul is fresh created in the developing embryo. St. Augustine was troubled on realizing that this fresh creation did not provide a clear mechanism for original sin to be inherited from Adam.

Jehovah's Witnesses are firmly attached to the Bible. In a pamphlet "*What is the soul?*" they also make clear that the soul has different meanings in the English translation of the Old and the New Testaments. In the former, "the human soul is not immortal": it was under Greek, not Christian, influence that the soul comes to be considered separate from the body

* It is interesting that the terms in Buddhist sources for 'soul' are *atman* (Pali); *atta* (Sanskrit), each of which means *breath*: in Greek the word is *pneuma*.

and as immortal.

Another group unprepared to depart from the Bible are the Christadelphians. In their pamphlet, "*Physical Resurrection*", T. J. Barling argues (cogently, I feel) that the Bible leaves little doubt that the Christian resurrection involves the raising of the body, its re-endowment with personality (the term used here, and by other writers, in preference to the many-faceted 'soul'), and its immortalization. This view has the notable practical advantage of conferring immortality only on those qualified for resurrection by appropriate Christian convictions. This appears to eliminate the problem of the disposal of the souls of those who have never even heard of Christianity, e.g., in India, China, America, etc., both before and after Christian missionaries first arrived in such countries. The state of limbo has been imaginatively created for these by the Roman and other churches. The Christadelphian model has the further advantageous simplification of excluding the question of the pre-existence of the soul before birth, and the question of the time of its entry into the human body. The absence of an element of immortality during the individual's life on earth would seem to be eminently reasonable from all practical experience, and even metaphysically acceptable.

The conferment of an immortal element (soul or personality) only at the resurrection of the body implies that even the Christian saints in this world have only been able to anticipate this status. It means we are all only potential soul acquirers. Excellent — perhaps irrefutable — as a practical proposition: but I cannot say whether it would now be generally acceptable as a part of Christian dogma. Certainly, this would not have been so in the past, nor is it so at present in the case of the Roman church. One recent commentator (K. Ward: *The Concept of God*; Blackwell, Oxford, 1974) has written: "In both the scientific and theological enterprises we have to be satisfied with models which are 'candidates for reality', which are reformable, and which are as close as we can approach to the reality with our given experimental limitations and conceptual resources." But how many believers are in this open-minded state?

Having made these few indications of present views on the soul in Christian circles, some readers might feel that has been an adequate synopsis. But the situation is not as simple as that might suggest. Owing to confusion in the Biblical texts themselves, leaving no clear view of the nature of the soul, Christian theologians have been free to speculate, and frequently they have pontificated, on the soul. That these views are not irrelevant today is seen from the controversies on abortion and, now more recently, on the permissible treatment of artificial (*in vitro*) foetuses. Much of the conservative protest in these matters (but not all) derives from much earlier, historically interesting, conceptions of the soul, its character, and its entry into the developing body

The persistent difficulty in seeking a Christian clarification of the soul is, as already stated, the lack of any, even brief consistent statement in the Bible. Many theologians have scanned the subject. In the Laidlow lectures at Toronto in 1959, Professor Pelikan summarizes the views of five early fathers of the Church: Tatian; Clement of Alexandria; Cyprian; Origen; Irenaeus.

With his teacher, Justin, Tatian declares unqualified opposition to the idea of the pre-existence of the soul as well as to its immortality.

Clement, by contrast, claims that the Christian elect existed before the foundation of the world and will survive its destruction. He accepts much from the Greeks pertaining to the soul. This source, rather than the Bible, provided the major basis for Christian views on the soul. He quotes Plato with approval: "For the harmony of the soul it is necessary to take care of the body", and adds, with a nice anticipation of the wordly Church: "By this, he who proclaims the message of truth is able to live, and to live well".

Cyprian writes of death as a consolation: it allows the faithful to enjoy the company of the saints. This view has provided untold consolation through the centuries.

Origen considered three possibilities for the soul:

(i) it is specially created and introduced into the body;
(ii) it is transmitted, like the body, from one generation to the next;
(iii) it pre-exists and comes into the body at an appropriate moment.

This last idea was declared anathema, and the second received no support.

And then Irenaeus offers a view of the soul combining

human and God-like qualities: the latter, in the form of immortality, giving it transcendent importance.

Finally, it was Socrates, as reported with approval by Plato, who averred that the philosopher (if no-one else) must be concerned with the soul, and not with the body. The Christian church made this Greek (not Judaic) proposition the centre of its teaching for more than fifteen hundred years. Many Christians would say it still does. The profound influence of this soul-emphasis in human affairs throughout the Christian centuries would only with difficulty be exaggerated. Many aspects of European history could be expounded on this basis. It has been an enormous delusion from which so many irrational, mortifying, calamitous consequences have arisen — and continue to do so.

Perhaps the best known, and certainly one of the major aspects of the Roman Church's doctrine of the soul stems from Fulgenius of Ruspe (467-533). He was a disciple of Augustine's and taught, not only that all unbaptized children but even those who die in their mother's womb are eternally damned. He held that all pagans, Jews, heretics, and schismatics who die outside the Catholic Church will go into the everlasting fire prepared for them. This prospect, so frequently preached and illustrated in the past, instilled a fear by no means dissipated today. It encouraged the niceties of the Spanish Inquisition in its methods to persuade heretics to join their church. The hell-fire pattern constituted the established thought of the Roman Church after it was confirmed explicitly by the Lateran Council (1215) and repeated at the Council of Ferrara and Florence (1438–39).

These views serve to show the range of opinions on the soul amongst the early fathers of the Church. However, another excellent guide is available on this question. The young Joseph Needham spent two years as a novitiate lay brother in the Oratory of the Good Shepherd, before entering on his biochemical studies at Cambridge. There he became a research director in the 1930s, with his major interest in the problems of understanding the development of the embryo from a fertilized egg. In this context he published a masterly three-volume work on *Chemical Embryology* (1931). The first 227 pages of Vol. 1 are devoted to a history of embryological studies. In this, the author was able to use directly sources in Greek, Latin,

Arabic, French, Italian, and German.

Much is revealed of the teaching *a propos* the appearance of the soul in the body. The importance of the soul and its relation to the body is established by the fact that so many of those who built up the corpus of Christian doctrine concerned themselves explicitly with this question. Terullian (*ca.* 160–230) one of the earliest Church fathers, held the soul was fully present in the embryo througout the pre-natal period. St. Augustine of Hippo (354–430) (not the St. Augustine who came to Canterbury) played a large role in welding Platonic teaching into Christian thought. He went so far as to decide the embryo was "besouled" in the second month, and "besexed" in the fourth. Abortion became homicide and punishable by death. Canon (Roman Church) law first ruled the soul arrived in male embryos on the 40th day, in female embryos on the 80th day. Further enlightenment arrived when it was decided that the 40th day applied to both sexes. The embryo, having acquired its soul, could be baptized *in utero*, St. Thomas Aquinas being of the opinion that such embryos might well be saved. (As far as I am aware, he did not clarify the form of life a three-month embryonic soul would have through eternity.) In treatises produced by the learned St. Hildegard (1098–1180), abbess at Bingen in the Rhineland, the soul is shown descending from heaven via a tube, into the embryo in the mother. There were doubts as to whether this regularly occurred, but another serious criticism was that this mechanism perhaps did not allow for original (i.e. Adam's) sin being transmitted from one generation to another.

Gradually, through the centuries, theological embryology faded into a quiescent state, only to be re-stimulated in the late twentieth century. The greater nonsense was forgotten (but not revoked) when it was generally accepted that, whatever the soul is, it cannot be perceived by the senses. This placed it safely and exclusively in the heads of the theologians and philosophers. Before this disappearance from common view, a notable practical flourish appeared in the report by Doctors of Divinity at the Sorbonne. In 1733 they published a firm recommendation that intra-uterine baptism of the soul-bearing embryo should be made by means of a syringe.

This cursory excursion into Christian sources shows how extraordiarily varied and confused is the doctrine on the soul.

Professor Pelikan in his survey writes: "Christianity has no doctrine of the soul; or, more precisely, it has several". It might well seem best to leave it: that, in fact, is what I intend to do, or, rather, to deviate from it and look at another closely related concept, immortality. Although it is not entirely correct, it is a very close approximation to the case, that the soul's all-essential role is that of being immortal. Coleridge, in one of his flashes of insight, in discussing this relation, put it very succinctly: "What is (immortality) but the impossibility of believing the contrary?" This comment is equally valid in its equivalent form: What is the soul but the impossibility of believing it non-existent?

The first thing to note about immortality is that the belief in it is extremely widespread. It is probable, however, that most people when they affirm a belief in immortality, are actually thinking of something much more limited: they have in mind survival after death for some finite time. The period of survival may well be related to that of human life, that is, it is (unconsciously?) anticipated in terms of decades or a few hundred years. Unfortunately, I have no evidence of the period which people wish, and therefore think, to be appropriate for their survival. Modern medicine has familiarized the public with "states of survival" in life which are equivalent to the death of the personality, but which can be maintained, artificially, for years. Few of those claiming some form of immortality in which communication with others will be possible would be happy with a period of, say, ten hours — as that would restrict them to contact only with those dying within an interval of twenty hours. Maybe one or two hundred years is what they have in mind? Certainly not a few thousand million years, although that is the age of the earth, and that astronomical period is itself a completely inexpressible minute (essentially zero) fraction of eternity.

Theologians and philosophers have made much of the almost universal belief in immortality. Something so strongly supported by opinion must have an element of truth? Further consideration leads to the suggestion that the idea could not be so widespread had it not come "from on high". That, at least, makes a consistent extension: both the concept and its origin are then transcendental, that is, beyond the range of experience. But the belief in immortality arises from an acceptance of the transcendental. The most pervasive experience we all share is that of being aware of ourselves, and of our continuing existence. Dreamless sleep, anaesthesia, other experiences of being unconscious, are all accepted as periods through which we have passed, but of which we have no communicable experience. We have no experience whatsoever of not being aware of ourselves. That is why it is extremely difficult, even with determined effort, for most people consciously to accept their future non-existence. They have no knowledge of such a state. It is to them transcendental, or at least, beyond experience.

The fear of the unknown is nowhere more completely illustrated than in the assumption of life after death.

There is one other, and obvious element, demanding belief in some form of immortality. One's closest relations — spouses, parents, maybe children, and so many friends, who all made life what it has been for each one of us and whom it is impossible to forget without having one's brain damaged — so many of these have departed this world. It requires the greatest of mental efforts to accept that they are for ever wiped away and that, with our own death, the memories of them will be beyond further recall. Hence the persistent thought, which becomes a belief, that a further meeting of some kind is the only thing which can compensate for the dukkha in this life, or that can "make sense of this world".

This, perhaps, is where the scientist has some minute advantage over others. He has been trained to accept nothing but what is based on demonstrable evidence. Some small experience in research will have taught him that, however much his own judgement favours a particular conclusion, if the facts are against it, then it must be abandoned. And there have been scientists almost as attached to their own theories as to their children. If they are scientists, and the facts fail to support their theory, then the theory has to go. Such is the price for putting truth first. Should the scientist not do so, he will soon be declared professionally bankrupt. I can sense many readers thoughts. They know of good scientists who confidently believe in immortality. Some such scientists may well be amongst the readers. What then? Nothing could be simpler. Please will they provide the observable evidence for survival after death?

At this stage, many will tell themselves: there are so many things science does not know. How true! The competent scientist is better aware than most of this limitation. The question is not of wishing to believe something beyond science: the question is, do we wish to believe something bearing none of the criteria of truth? This restriction is unbearable for many. They will go free: with no acceptable constraints on imaginative conclusions. Not only the western world has been plagued and plundered by spiritualists. With the B.B.C. lending its hand to all sorts of fallacious sorcery, it is too much to hope that innocent people will not be further duped.

Llewelyn Powys, perhaps the least appreciated of the three writer-brothers Powys, an acutely sensitive person who, for thirty years, managed to survive killer attacks of tuberculosis, wrote his judgement:* "Let us once again repeat the actual truth of the case, that hopeless, dangerous truth which the human race is everywhere, and at all times, so reluctant to acknowledge. All religions, all metaphysical systems, all cogging theories of life that claim for human polity any foundation outside the ramparts of the visible world, are the veriest counterfeits . . . As a spider suspends herself by ropes from her own body, so the human race has created out of its head imaginary meshes that through a kind of hallucination of mass-faith acquires the appearance of substance."

This is a strong statement. Can it be justified? Well, despite the uncertainty as to the nature of the soul, can we agree on some minimum requisite for a meaningful form of survival after death?

I wish to suggest there are two requisites of which the first is an essential, and the second will be accepted as meaningful and almost essential. To have a significant form of survival, the entity which avoids death (let us call it 'the spirit') must be able to recognize that it has survived and is aware of its own identity. In simple terms, the spirit must be, in some degree, conscious of its own identity. To negate this feature would be to have a spirit devoid of any possible relation to the person from whom it has derived and as characterless as an invisible balloon of hot air.

The second feature is that the spirit should be able to

---

* Llewelyn Powys, *Impassioned Clay*, Longmans, Green: 1931, p. 105

communicate by some means with other similar spirits. Maybe this ability to communicate (as, indeed, also the self-identification) would have to be acquired in the next world, just as a new-born child has to do in this world. Although the spirit could exist without this second requisite, it would then only lead an aimless, wandering existence. I am tempted to suggest that this first, minimum spirit, would be in a state close to that described (insofar as it can be described, and I am able to appreciate it) by the Buddhists as nibbana. Such a state might be so enthralling that the isolated, non-communicating spirit would continue (for a thousand million years?) in a happy glow of self-satisfaction? Or, perhaps in a state of acute dissatisfaction?

With the addition of the power to communicate, the spirit will, we must assume, contact other similar spirits: messages can be exchanged and, maybe, memories accumulated in the other world. This, it seems to me, is the minimum which could make survival, perhaps, barely acceptable. Certainly, many will be persuaded that much more should be, or can be, or is, achieved in the next world. I am in no position even to wish to restrict their imaginations. I am merely anxious to minimize what might be called "the necessary structure" in the spirit world. To ask for messages to be transmissible to this world, is to require much greater development and elaboration in the character of the spirit. It may be appropriate to call this third stage a fully-gifted spirit.

Our first feature requires some degree of self-consciousness on the part of the spirit. If we look at the whole range of life forms, both at present and through the geological past, it is clear that self-awareness is well developed in the "higher", i.e., more complex animals, and is probably present in far more primitive organisms. As far as our human knowledge goes, the simplest state of self-awareness requires the organization of a structured nervous system. So we come to the question, how is this to be made available in the spirit world?

Our bodies visibly decay at death, a process much accelerated to its final stages by cremation. It is obvious that the spirit can only acquire its self-awareness if some special act of creation occurs after death. Obviously this is what soul-believing Christians aver, and many of like mind will ask why am I spelling out this requirement when they "know" that this miracle operates to install spirits in the next world. Well, they do not "know": they imagine or they are persuaded, as by a magician, that the physically impossible happens.

To produce spirits of the second (communicating) type, much more elaborate physical reconstruction would be needed, with vision or other senses well developed.

Many will think me (quite rightly?) very stupid. Why cannot I see that God (the being for whom there is no detectable evidence) operates this system: which, in any case, only occurs in "another" world, for which there is no evidence. By placing God and the spirits in a world apart, by that very location, it follows we can have no knowledge of them. The believers should now recur to Llewlyn Powys's statement.

I am only too painfully aware that many of my friends, and several of them scientists, accept this miraculous operation of the spirit world. It is where faith comes in. *Credo quia impossible:* I believe because it is impossible. At this point, reasoned discussion breaks down.

Is it necessary to remind the reader that the whole vast body of science and , in particular, the totality of the extraordinarily detailed quantitative knowledge we have of the physical universe and the biological world is based on the *assumption* that there is an undeviating regularity and that a coherent unity constantly prevails. The assumption is (or, has so far always been) found to be correct. The mass of evidence for it is as large as science itself. Miracles are not observed to occur. Even such unexpected happenings as Yuri Geller purported to demonstrate, are false.

In planning and achieving almost pin-point precision of landing on the moon, the essential dynamics of the vehicle were calculated by Newtonian mechanics. Those simple laws are amply accurate even in inter-planetary space where the Christian angels lived for many centuries. They have left for "the other world" before the arrival of the twentieth century. No minute residual field has been detected from their one-time presence. No miracles occur. As far as I am aware, even the most enthusiastic spiritualist who has "seen" objects moved by spirits, and much else, trusts himself to engine drivers or jet pilots whose journeys proceed on the assumption not only that the spirits will not touch a button, but that miracles do not occur.

In all this I realize I am merely saying why, being a scientist, it is not only impossible for me to support the hypothesis of an immortal or even briefly surviving soul, but that, as far as I am aware, such belief is fully equivalent to belief in miracles. Many people believe in miracles, that is, in the suspension or over-riding of the whole basis of science and of all repeatable observations. What can be done to dissuade them? Would any form of reasoned argument only make them more irrational?

There are no miracles, but there are close approximations to these strictly unknown phenomena. Observers do not agree on the number of instances but many would claim their occurrence in works by Mozart and Schubert. What adds significance to these cases is the fact that the phenomena are reproducible at almost any time or place, and have been so established for up to two centuries. The effect is generally experienced as that of being carried so far from the normal atmosphere of this earth's affairs as to be almost free from its inescapable environment: it is certainly sublime but "miraculous" here is a figure of speech.

Reason clearly plays a very large role in science. Some, less correctly, would say 'logic', or 'a critical common sense'. But whilst reason must not be abandoned in science — and some of its mathematical forms are distinctly uncommon — there in no need to indulge in the illusion that scientists, any more than anyone else, always behave rationally. Although he must have had 'reasons' ample to himself, most of us were perhaps surprised to learn the Einstein* never wore socks. What is essential to remember is that little in science survives that is not 'reasonable' in terms of fairly well-established results. Science has extended its realm by the application of reason to wider and newer fields. With large margins of uncertainty, this extension by rational analysis has also penetrated that very irrational area, human behaviour. Even in history, Robert Briffault's brilliant volume of 1919 (ante-dating Wells's *History of the World), The making of Humanity,* makes a strongly argued case that progress in (Western) civilization had been commen-

---

* One of his extraordinarily concise, significant statements took the form: When I am asked to believe some of the commonly accepted religio-philosophic opinions, I feel I am being asked to swallow something which I do not have in my mouth.

surate with the application of reason. Perhaps the history of this century might be taken to illlustrate the converse process.

There is no reason to claim there is life after death. The belief, however, gives enormous comfort to so many, but why be happy with an illusion? There is, of course, a small industry not now looked upon so disparagingly as in calmer times, providing messages "from the other world". As far as I am aware, these messages are not received or reproduced under any controlled conditions, nor are they publicly demonstrated. If they were, we should surely be striving for some authentic exchanges with — well, what a choice we have! Two well-known spiritualists who undertook to communicate from "the next world" were Sir Arthur Conan Doyle and Sir Oliver Lodge. Doubtless someone has "heard" from them. But how many who knew them well have been able to share this much-sought-after experience?

We must all remain open to conviction: which does not mean that we suspend judgement on what is already established. Many thousands of millions of humans have died, and yet there is no consistent or reproducible evidence of anything but the minutest fraction even attempting to communicate with this world. All organisms or systems able to send self-controlled messages have a substantial material structure and the equivalent of an integrated nervous system. It requires a miracle for the buried or cremated dead of this world to acquire that. There is no limit to what the imagination can suppose to happen in the hypothetical "next world" — perhaps we could be enlarged butterflies, as the angels have been depicted? Nothing but illusion is so created. For the sake of truth, may reason prevail.

What does Buddhism say in this context? The answer is: you can take your choice. Far and away the largest part, that is the Mahayana school, offers all the features of an elaborate spirit world. The state of being in the other world is fully described in its various levels, and the time-scale of survival is truly generous — some tens of millions of years. Furthermore, in many sects, "communication" with the next world is on a fairly regular basis. Established ceremonies and proper incantations can produce immediate results. Much blowing of conches, beating of drums and other means of generating impressively large sound is found to help the arrival and the signalling of many spirits, but the message is usually received only by those suitably trained and having a sensitive "inner ear". Many tens of millions are happy sustainers of such experiences, which make the anaemic whispers of Western spiritualists and the "still small voice" of Judaeo-Christian practices pale into insignificance. A sad limitation to these striking manifestations is that no-one can be assured of any benefit in substance from the experience: merely "an up-lift of spirit". The powerful, age-long necromancy of the Tantric Buddhists does not appear to have given them any advantage of a material kind, or even a better understanding of this world. How sad that the spirits, endowed with truly fantastic powers and experiences, prove to be so unhelpful. We must do better in the West.

The reader is, however, already aware that this present approach to Buddhism is very much confined to the Theravada school. The Theravadins have a very different stance. They are explicitly clear that there is no soul. Interestingly enough, many, if not most, of the Western students of Buddhism, until well into this century, refused to accept that the Theravadins denied the existence of the soul. Coming on top of the Tathagata's insistence that he neither knew nor found it profitable to discuss the existence of a Supreme Being, this further scepticism was difficult to swallow. Especially so, for those brought up on Plato.

It is the Theravadin scholars themselves who insist on the no-soul position. Walpola Rahula writes (in summarizing statements from the Pali sources) ". . . the Buddha denied categorically, in unequivocal terms, in more that one place, the existence of Atman, Soul, Self, or Ego within men or without, or anywhere else in the universe." Similar statements come in other expositions of Theravada teaching. In E. J. Thomas's *Life of the Buddha,* he specifically refers to one occasion when the Tathagata discoursed on the non-existence of the soul: he commenced, "The body, monks, is soul-less." (ibid. p.88).

The basis of this negative conclusion is clear. Gotama repeatedly presented an analysis of the soul or the self (often no distinction is insisted upon between these two concepts). The analysis is into five aspects, called aggregates. Each of these aspects are "conditioned", that is, they are variable features so that the self or soul has no permanent, defined character. And there is no question of anything other than these variable elements being present in "the soul". Also, this constantly fluctuating entity is not immortal: "all conditioned entities are impermanent".

Strangely enough, even the Mahayana teaching accepts the no-soul thesis. The spirits so prominently present in these other schools are more in the nature of disembodied humans: perhaps one could say 'ghosts'. They likewise have a finite life.

There are, however, notable inconsistencies in the Theravada position. Denying the existence of a permanent soul, it nevertheless accepts a fully structured spirit world. By 'structured' one means a world in which spirits of various status exist and interact, both with themselves and with the real world. This is an enormous incongruity when it is claimed that the Tathagata himself insisted that belief should be withheld from any proposition which cannot be tested by experience. There is some doubt whether the "supremacy of reason" thesis did not more strongly prevail in early Buddhist teaching. Certainly it was soon relaxed in favour of the spirit world. Possibly — indeed, it seems probable — it came about from an overwhelming pressure based on the dominance of spirit-entities in the contemporary Brahminical-Hindu world of the sixth and later centuries B.C.

Another major obscurity arises when one asks: accepting that there is no permanent or identifiable element to be called the soul or the self, what is it that is carried from one life to be reborn in another? The belief in rebirth has been as wiedspread in Buddhism as the soul is in Christianity. In the one case, the whole aim is to avoid rebirth by achieving nibbana: in the other, it is to ensure the salvation of the soul as the preparation for heaven. (At least, that is what used to be the Christian aim.)

The Buddhist reply is in no way convincing. We are told that the individual embodies five varying aggregates, not themselves permanent: but that, in an individual they generate a pattern, a focus (of energy?), a character, a field of force — many alternatives are expressed — and that it is this entity which passes from the dying person to one newly being born. It seems the entity may spend some time before being attached to a new birth.

The idea seems to be to postulate a conservation of individual life-experiences. The pattern of aggregates which is transitorily present in the dying person becomes transferred to a new physical body. This also accounts for the fact that Buddhists all believe that, given sufficient progress on the way to enlightenment, each one of us would be able to recall our previous existence, that is, the record of good and evil previously achieved.

All this is the merest speculation. No evidence, that I am aware of, exists to confirm the rebirth hypothesis. If reason is to make judgement, it must be unreservedly rejected. In Buddhism as expounded in the early (and modern) texts, the rebirth is essential in that the aim of nibbana corresponds to its cessation. However, there is what we might call a consistency of negatives here. Nibbana is itself characterized as "beyond description": and it is now seen to involve a certain fiction, rebirth. My conclusion is that, apart from historical interests, they should both be forgotten.

By streching one's imagination, one can offer some analogy to the balance of kamma with which the Buddhist believes one arrives in this world. This can be supposed to correspond to the collection of genes we each inherit from our parents, and, more distantly, from our ancestors. We do not start out equal, as the congenitally blind, mongols, spinabifidas, etc., so dramatically and painfully remind us. We are compounded from our ancestors. We are not, be it noted, related except on some rare chance, to anyone who has died immediately before our birth.

Buddhism, by incorporating concepts current in the Indian world, has, in these instances saddled itself with much that is meaningless. What is remarkable, is that there should be so small an element of unreality in the Tathagata's teaching. In rejecting the rebirth thesis, the only loss is to those who would accept the teaching only because it could lead to the cessation of rebirths. Otherwise, nothing is lost by losing a non-event: but huge slices of Buddhist apologetics and commentaries pass into limbo: and the air is much clearer for their disappearance.

As a philosophy committed to the acceptance of the criteria of evidence, there seems to be no reason why Buddhism — in the Theravada form — should not accept the major conclusions of science. An exposition of those conclusions is only convincing when accompanied by the massive, often quantitative, evidence on which they are based. This is not the point at which to launch into a compendium of modern science, but it is not unreasonable to recall two general conclusions.

The first has already been indicated. The universe we observe has been moving to its present state for at least six thousand million years. We already know it to contain extraordinary structures (globular clusters, nebulae, white dwarfs, super-novae, quasars, black holes, etc.) but we must not imagine that our present knowledge is anything like complete. What the layman may not always appreciate is that these features are often more remarkable than anyone could have imagined — until the evidence for them had been consistently recorded. Most importantly, they can all be described in terms of mathematical physics which keeps expanding its concepts to account for them — but does not, by its nature, involve any miracles. And it is now being realized that this universe may be given a "geometry" such that its development is self-created. But no-one should suggest that by 2000 A.D. we will know all the essentials of the story.

The second major conclusion was brilliantly illustrated by David Attenborough's *Life on Earth*. Over some three thousand million years, the almost incredible variety of life forms have gradually increased in their variety of form and complexity of behaviour. Much of the evidence for this development is accessible to the layman in geological and natural history museums. Consideration of the physico-biolgical-environmental causes which can best explain the pattern of evolution is not here in any way needed. What is relevant is the fact that life *has* gradually assumed these multifarious forms over a huge span of time. To deny this is to stand with Galileo's contemporaries who could deny the existence of the moons of Jupiter because they refused to look through a telescope.

In this slow development of life forms, two legged, upright, walking creatures are found to have lived about three million years ago. Palaeontologists and anatomists are satisfied that the skeletal remains found in East Africa foreshadow the emergence of what we call *homo sapiens*. There are many details and a very long chain of specimens, coming nearer to us in time, which justify this profoundly important conclusion. No-one responsibly suggests that the whole picture is clear, but there is an accumulation of very critically assessed material evidence which cannot be convincingly interpreted other than by accepting that the specimens represent stages in the slow emergence of humans.

This pattern (which Macaulay would have introduced "As every schoolboy knows") has its doubters. It is not acceptable (or was not until very recently) for teaching in the schools of Mississippi, Tennessee and some other southern states of the U.S.A. And much nearer home, in Catholic countries, it is a rather hot potato.

The Catholic Commentary on Holy Scripture (1953) makes the situation plain. I quote. "It was not the wish of the Holy Ghost, in inspiring the sacred writers, to teach such matters of purely secular knowledge. This applied also to the theory — it is nothing more than a theory lacking proof — that the human body has been evolved from lower forms. If it should ever be established, the religious teaching of Genesis would remain the same . . . That man has a spiritual rational soul is established by philosophy, as is also the fact that such a spiritual substance could not have its origin in anything material. And it is due to man's spiritual soul that his mental powers differ essentially from those of even the highest of the brute creation."

"Pius XII reminds us that the question does not belong exclusively to the field of natural sciences and that the sources of revelation impose caution and moderation. It is one that may be freely discussed, provided we are prepared to accept the decision of the Church to whom Christ committed the charge of interpreting Holy Scripture and of guarding the doctrines of the Faith." (Human genesis: AAS 42(1950) 575 f.)

This is admirably clear. There is no reason why one should not accept it if one agrees to have one's options decided by the doctors of the Church. Not to put too heavy a hand on it, those soul-controlling doctors (strictly, the *Italian* Inquisition) obliged Galileo to swear the earth did not move around the sun. Pope John Paul has recanted that view. We conclude that the Catholic doctors may again (how frequently?) be wrong.*

How much I appreciate the statement in the Catholic Commentary on Holy Scripture. The Roman Church, at least,

* See page 134.

defines where it stands, even though it be without foundation. My guess is that a whole enormously blurred spectrum of views would come from the Anglican Church: and nothing much better from most others. But to their credit, the non-Roman churches would allow each person to examine the evidence and arrive at his/her own, albeit mistaken (?), conclusions.

Why is the long, slow evolution of man from lower forms of the "brute creation" such a hot potato? Well, for at least two obvious reasons. Firstly, it enormously contrasts with the Biblical story of a special creation of the world and then of man in it. Most Judaeo-Christian-Moslems are now reconciled to the falsity of the special creation thesis. It is felt to be unnecessary and the Holy Ghost, insofar as that entity was involved, must be credited with a dubious performance: not, of course, for the last time.

The more troublesome aspect arises when one asks, at what stage in the evolution of humans did the soul appear? Remember Aquinas?: no humans without a soul. With Neanderthal man: Beijing man: Australopithecus: Homo habitis: etc.? Perhaps the soul grew with the size of the brain or with the creature's powers of reason? Or (heretical thought) is the soul only potentially present in each of us and only in the properly disposed believer does it grow into significance? For those who wish not to dispose of the soul concept, I suggest this is a helpful hypothesis. It matches well the behaviour of the Christian conquerors of South America. These were permitted to slaughter the brutes of human form until they had converted them to the knowledge of having a

---

* It is worth quoting precisely what the Committee of Cardinals forming the Congregation of the Index wrote of Copernicus's thesis that, rather than the sun and the heavens moving around the earth, the earth actually spun on its axis and revolved around the sun. In a decree of the congregation of the Index, dated March 5, 1616, the work of Copernicus was suspended: *Falsam illam doctrinam Pythagoricam, divinae quae Scripturae omino adversantem, de mobilitate Terrae et immobilitate Solis.* This false doctrine of Pythagoras (being advanced by Copernicus) absolutely opposed to the Holy Scriptures, concerning the mobility of the earth and the immobility of the sun.

A later (1620) dish of the Cardinals' sauce describes Copernicus's book "As repugnant to the Holy Scriptures and its true and Catholic interpretation [for] he does not hesitate to treat [of his subject] *by hypothesis,* but he even adds [of it] "*as most true*". (The emphasis is that of the princes of the Roman Church).

The same bizarre negations can be seen in current Catholic statements on birth control and other topics.

soul which, almost simultaneously, was saved by the Church. As the present-day descendants of the Quetchuan Indians of the Inca empire insist, they have never recovered from this conversion. And the potential soul hypothesis allows for all those, the great majority of humans, in China and other countries, who have, throughout history and even today, not heard of the true religion and are quite unaware that they might have, or might cultivate, eternal souls.

Whilst we can assume that all serious modern writers on philosophy and religion are amply aware of the scale and age and generally non-human character of the universe, and also equally aware of the extraordinary aeons-long evolution of life forms leading to the slow emergence of the human species, — whilst they know of these observations, they so frequently proceed to discuss human problems and beliefs as though the story in Genesis provided a valid background.

Many will feel I exaggerate, and that I show excessive concern to reiterate the major conclusions of science. The reading of letters in *The Times* over a period of some six months would, I think, validate my concern. On questions ranging from abortion, and *in vitro* or *in vivo* foetuses, to the appointment of a Bishop of Durham (who does not appear to believe in the virgin birth or the bodily resurrection of Christians) one finds legal luminaries, eminent churchmen, highly educated laymen, *et al.* all writing almost as their predecessors would have four hundred years ago. By the time the television chat-shows have added their own spectrum of opinion-jockeys' and housewives' views, the general public is in a finely confused state of mind — ready to absorb the following morning's astrological mumbo-jumbo. With that opiate, the public mind is finally conjured back four centuries.

A responsible scientist might almost be defined as one who is constantly aware of the uncertainties of detail in his deductions, but no outlook which does not accept the broad conclusions of science can do other than create the same delusions as the flat-earth theorists. Our educational system seems almost incapable of establishing a rational position.

A final quotation on the immortal soul: "By what arguments or analogies can we prove any state of existence, which no one ever saw, and which no way resembles any that ever was seen? . . . Some new species of logic is requisite for that purpose, and some new faculties of the mind, that they may enable us to comprehend that logic."

"Nothing could set in a fuller light the infinite obligations which mankind have to Divine revelation, since we find no other medium could ascertain this great and important truth." Thus, with incomparable irony, wrote David Hume.

Amongst philosophers, this question has been regarded as largely closed since Hume wrote. Why, then, pursue it here? Very simply, because so many serious minded people are still more than uncertain on the question. In one form or another, often in some ineffably vague form, they still retain a belief in immortality. This polarizes their outlook. A major crack in the foundations of a house will not contribute to its safety or stability: although, it must be admitted many such do survive a lifetime, showing signs of their uncertain base only in their interiors. To the Tathagata we can give the credit for being so clear-headed, where almost all other religious leaders and so many philosophers have been bemused.

Confucius, too, refused to be drawn into any transcendental aspects of an after life. The rather large fraction of the human race found in China have generally been immune to such illusion. They have certainly "worshipped" their ancestors: that is, they have ceremoniously recalled their memories and shown respect for their achievements and views. But that is an altogether more mundane and realistic an activity.

The Theravada teaching makes two related claims.

1. There is no permanent, abiding self or ego, or immortal soul.

2. There is, however, a tenuous form of transmigration from one human to another. It is thought of as some flame or pattern of consciousness which passes from the dying to a new born child. This residue of Brahminical-Hindu belief has been retained to give substance to the cycle of rebirths. For this there is as much evidence as for the immortal soul. In accepting it, Gotama made a major departure from his insistence that belief should follow only what can be demonstrated or shown to apply. As the Theravada teaching is not a religion, there is no need even for Theravadins to accept it.

The Emperor Asoka

Asoka's name has already been mentioned several times. His significance in the history of Buddhism is such that a very brief account of his role is called for.

Archaeology shows that the early high level of civilization achieved by the natives of the Indus valley in North-west India in their cities at Mohenjo-Dara and Harappa went into decline simultaneously with the arrival of the Aryans around 1700 B.C. The Aryans entered as conquering hordes: they came from the area to the east of the Caspian Sea (the Hindu Kush). This is relevant as it made them lighter skinned than the natives they found in India and the conqueror/subject relation was the early basis of the caste system. The warriors, the priests, the craftsmen and trades people of Aryan origin tended to remain aloof from the farming and labouring native Indians. Although the groups were not at first rigidly defined, this development was fostered by the priestly Brahmins who elevated themselves through the cult of ceremonies and sacrifices so as to achieve a status even superior to that of the warriors.

Asoka was the third Mauryan emperor (269–232 B.C.). His grandfather ruled not only great areas of the Indus and Ganges valleys but also much to the north, including most of what is now Afghanistan. Extended by his father, Asoka added even further to the empire until it embraced almost the whole of India apart from the area south of a line approximately Madras-Bangalore. Not for two thousand years was the sub-continent to be so largely unified.

Asoka made his new conquests early in his reign. After one campaign involving great loss of life, he did more even than Wellington in expressing horror at the senseless waste. He abandoned the role of conquering warrior and accepted the teaching of Buddha. He did not abandon his position as emperor, but he ruled with an enlightenment which made him a figure of great appeal.

During Asoka's reign, the third Buddhist council was called. This is credited with the formulation of the teaching, and from it the major historic version of Buddhism derives in the form of the Pali canon of the Theravada school. At the same time differences of belief and interpretation crystallized into diverging sects. What is now found as the Mahayana form was given a separate role, distinct from the more strictly historic and rational Theravadin's. The far more liberal, imaginative, and openly religious beliefs of the new Mahayana community thenceforward has its own detailed history, which will be briefly related later. Asoka is reported to have been perturbed by the differences which proved irreconcilable, and to have promoted the expulsion of the dissidents.

Indian history attains a documented state in Asoka's time. His commitment to Buddhism is established in numerous records which are still publicly extant: most of all, in inscribed pillars scattered over the whole of his extensive empire. Only as recently as 1895 was one of the many pillars recognized in a Nepalese village. The inscription is in the Magadhi language and states that Asoka in the fourteenth year of his reign had caused an early stupa (artificial mound) commemorating the Buddha to be doubled in size and, in the twentieth year of his reign, had himself visited the spot to pay his respects. The following year another pillar, also in Nepal, was found with the inscription, which translated reads:

'When King Asoka had been annointed twenty years, he came himself and worshipped (at this spot), because the Buddha Sakyamuni was born here. He both caused to be made a stone bearing a horse (?a lion?); and caused a stone pillar to be set up (in order to show) that the Blessed One was born here. (He) made the village of Lumbini free of taxes, and paying (only) an eighth part of the produce.'

A temple now marks this traditional birthplace. The two pillars clearly refer to actual visits of Asoka. At Kandabar, Asoka left inscriptions in both Greek and Aramaic.

Asoka had inherited an empire already well organized with a centralized bureaucracy, His acceptance of Buddhism gave it an official ideology. He is credited with promoting the erection of tens of thousands of Buddhist temples but, whilst he strongly promoted Buddhism, he did not attempt to thrust it upon those of another persuasion. He was, in fact, generous in support of the Jains and the Brahman-Hindus. Asoka antedated Napoleon by more than two thousand years. His empire was far the more extensive. In his youth he had been a ruthless autocrat and the autocracy still remained. The use he made of his unlimited powers, throughout his twenty-eight years reign, shows an enlightenment unique amongst the rulers of the world.

Asoka's rock and pillar inscriptions spelt out a complete socially-inclined Buddhist doctrine for the lay person. He proclaims respect for the dignity of all men, and for all forms of life: religious tolerance is commended and violence in all forms abhorred. Animal sacrifices are prohibited (which caused great concern and, later, opposition from the Brahmins: it is still not enforced in many Indian communities). His guidance was usually in general terms and called for the co-operation of the individual and the community. Charity, good works, justice and honesty were to be cultivated. He gave official status to panels of examiners of behaviour (morals): that undue, unhealthy, advantage was taken by members of these panels is not surprising. Not all his subjects were good Buddhists, although in one inscription Asola claimed (was he the first to project such an all-embracing responsibility?) "All people are my children".

Best remembered by his subjects were Asoka's public works of benevolence. Along the roads through the empire he caused banyan trees to be planted. Not only are these fig trees associated with the Buddha, but with their aerial roots that find the ground to spread the tree over great areas, they provide highly welcome shade from the relentless heat of the Indian sun. Their presence helped to guide the traveller along his route, where, for the first time, rest-houses were also now provided at short intervals. Asoka undertook the systematic inprovement of water resources, having wells and irrigation canals dug throughout his domains. Homes for the sick were provided: even, it seems, 'hospitals' for animals. To assist in the treatment of the sick, herb gardens were to be regularly cultivated.

According to one inscription Asoka proclaimed: "There is no such giving of help as the giving of the dhamma", i.e., the gift of Gotama's teaching. This injunction has been compared with that of a notably practical and successful western leader. Oliver Comwell wrote: "Building of hospitals provides for men's bodies; to build temples is judged a work of piety; but they that procure spiritual food, they that build up spiritual temples, they are the men truly charitable, truly pious". Asoka was clearly committed to charity and piety.

In his administration Asoka created departments whose aims

reflected his enlightenment. Apart from the supervision of charitable works, one "ministry" was to care for the subject races and for the aboriginal peoples, previously left to their primitive existence. Education was to be fostered: his inscriptions are the public records of this concern, which also was specifically extended to women. These aspects of his policy were repugnant to the Brahmins, and likely to be destructive to the caste system. They did not, of course, succeed in that respect.

Although Asoka first embraced Buddhism as a lay person, he is said later to have entered the sangha, i.e., the order of monks: but this must have been as a "honorary member". He could not have continued his reign from the seclusion of a monastry. His limited, or controlled, commitment to Buddhist doctrine is, perhaps, seen in the absence of any mention of nibbana in his inscriptions. Maybe, this characterizes his acceptance of Buddhism as a pragmatic philosophy, fully relevant for this world, whether or not it impinged on another? Although it is wildly unreasonable to doubt his acceptance of the essentials of the Tathagata's teaching, historians have been pleased to indicate how entirely beneficial Asoka's actions were for maintaining peace and for promoting prosperity throughout his empire of many races all with diverse religions and cultural attachments. That they imply his enlightenment might have had a purely pragmatic basis is, of course, a profound if unintended commendation of Buddhism. It is a welcome admission of how truly effective the Buddha's teaching becomes when practised with conviction by those in power.

Asoka's commitment to Buddhism is sealed beyond doubt by his missionary ventures. Up to his time Buddhism had been largely confined to its original home, the provinces of north-east India. Not only was it now, by royal decree, spread through the sub-continent, but it was taken by special missions to Burma, to Sri Lanka, to Macedonia and to Egypt. In the first two countries it became permanently established in the Theravada form. The Sri Lankan mission was especially important. It was led by Asoka's son, Mahinda. and six companions. Endowed with imperial prestige, they had little problem converting the king (Tissa) and many of the Sri Lankan nobility. So sweeping was their success that a second mission, headed by one of Asoka's daughters, arrived to establish communities of Buddhist nuns. Despite this very favourable initiation, Buddhism has had a chequered career in Sri Lanka. A most important role there has been that it produced one of the earliest recordings of Buddhist teaching in Pali, a source already repeatedly mentioned.

Exchanges of Buddhist teachers between Sri Lanka and Burma continued through the centuries. Burmese missions more than once came to Sri Lanka to help re-invigorate failing Buddhist practices. From Burma also, Buddhism spread into Cambodia and Thailand, in both of which it has remained dominant and, again, largely in the Theravada form.

At the courts of the Seleucids and the Ptolemies Asoka's missionaries had much smaller success. Their influence, though small, can, it seems, be traced in the contemporary records. Greeks were amongst the converts in Egypt.

No leader in India's history came near the status of Asoka until Mahatma Gandhi in this century. But Ghandi's India, like the Mahatma himself, was Hindu. Buddhism in the Mahayana form, accepted many elements of Hinduism and, in so far as it resisted such infiltration, it was constantly frowned upon by the Brahmins. It fell into disrepute and gradually faded almost completely from the Indian scene. Few features of Buddhism are clearly established in modern India but two can be recognised. Near the mound (stupa) built at Sarnath to commemorate Gotama's first sermon, Asoka erected one of his many columns. It carries one of his Buddhist inscriptions, in this case particularly censuring schismatic tendencies. The pillar is crowned by a stone drum supported on an inverted lotus carrying four magnificent lions, facing the corners of the world. This headstone is the established emblem of the Republic of India. Secondly, the constitution of the republic itself claims that its foreign policies will be based on five specific principles: all of which could well be claimed to be derived from the Buddhist principles applied in Asoka's administration. The five principles of India's foreign policy are known as *Panchasila* (Five Precepts or Virtues) and this, itself, is a Buddhist term.

To his contemporaries Asoka was "The beloved of the gods". Two things can be said of H. G. Wells's account of Buddhism and Asoka. Like much else in the *Outline of History*, it brought a new vision into world history (resented though much of it was by the professional historians). The chapter on

Buddhism must be one of the first adequate descriptions to reach a wide English readership. And one can, at least, appreciate the enthusiasm of the great humanist, that Wells was, for one of his favourite historical figures. "For eight and twenty years Asoka worked sanely for the real needs of men. Amidst the tens of thousands of names of monarchs that crowd the columns of history, their majesties and graciousnesses and serenities and royal highnesses and the like, the name of Asoka shines, and shines almost alone, a star. From the Volga to Japan his name is still honoured. China, Tibet, and even India, though it has left his doctrine, preserve the tradition of his greatness. More living men cherish his memory today than have ever heard the names of Constantine or Charlemagne."*

Mahayana Buddhism

What has thus far been considered in this account are essentially the elements of Theravada Buddhism. There is good reason to accept that it reflects more closely than any other form of Buddhism what was the personal teaching of Gotama. All the other schools use texts which, to an overwhelming degree, are much later in origin than the Pali tripitaka (three baskets). These other versions all expound beliefs and practices of which no trace can be found in earlier sources. The most important, because it is the most widespread, of all the later versions of Buddhism is that of the Mahayana school. This spread to Central Asia, China, Japan, Java, Sumatra and even back to Sri Lanka. It has remained far and away the largest of the divisions of Buddhism.

It is probably correct to say of the Mahayana school that it does not reject the core of the Theravada teaching: what it insists upon is that the latter is too narrow and too inadequate a version of the doctrine. The Mahayana is a truly inflated form, the very name means "the great vehicle" (*maha* is from the same root as our *major*). It may help if I attempt an indication of what promoted this expanded teaching.

The teaching of Gotama was given to a community profoundly interested in the transcendental. Whilst the high-

* The amazing disregard in the West for Eastern history is illustrated by *Chambers Biographical Dictionary* (1982). This gives fourteen words to Asoka, and more than four times that to the inventor of the Kipp's gas apparatus.

born Greeks were concerned with philosophy, one has the impression that religion was the staple diet of the Indian peoples. Almost contemporaneously with Gotama, the Vedic culture settled in to a pattern which has since been known as Hinduism. Then, as now, Hinduism represented an approach which tends to offer all things to all persons. Certainly it had an ample panoply of greater and lesser deities, abiding in a multitude of different existences. Against this imaginatively colourful background, Theravada Buddhism must have appeared to most people as a coldly austere, unattractive philosophy.

One distinctly convincing criticism of early Buddhism was its preoccupation with the individual and his attainment of nibbana, the prospects for which were enhanced by withdrawal into a monastic community. From the earliest councils, the view was expressed that such individual concern was narrow minded, that the aim should be to spread the benevolence of Gotama's teaching to the widest audience in a generous all-embracing approach. The contrast between the two early Buddhist streams was that between the subdued realism of the Theravada (called by its critics the Hinayana, i.e., the lesser vehicle), and the unrestrained openness of the Mahayana. Such a brief characterization of the distinction is over-simple, but indicates the general pattern.

The Mahayana schools (it must be emphasized there are very many different sects under the one general umbrella) lean principally on the early Sanskrit sources for their origination. Some of these are at least as old as the Pali texts of the Theravada, but it is from expositions deliberately composed centuries later — mostly after 200 A.D. that the Mahayana take their characteristic teaching. They do not at any stage deny the historical Gotama, or his records, but he is regarded as only one of a host of similarly inclined teachers, nearly all of whom are fictional creations often wandering through aeons of time and a multiplicity of creations. "The Mahayana does in fact multiply the number of Buddhas indefinitely and quite logically, since it is the goal of every individual to become a Buddha". It is difficult and almost pointless for me to continue beyond this revelation. All these Buddhas are worshipped and we are at an immense separation from the restrained rational outlook of the Theravadins, and are now faced with an unrestrained, mythological and polytheistic religion.

Writing from a Mahayana position and with a great knowledge of the sources, Conze wrote in one of his books: "Knowledge of the non-historical Buddhas seems to have grown as time went on. Originally there were seven, then we hear of twenty-four, and so the number increased." It is a novel use of the term "knowledge", to find that, given time, it can increase in the form of purely imaginary fictions. But that is not all. Given the "eye of faith", the Mahayana disciple can see things differently from the commonplace. Conze explained: "Our description of the Buddha would be incomplete if we failed to mention that alone among mortals of this age He had in addition to His normal physical body . . . still a kind of "ethereal" body which only the elect could see with the eye of faith . . . The "ethereal" body is sixteen feet high, and it possesses the thirty-two "marks of the superman"." The capitalization of He and His tells us we have arrived in the realm of religion. The fantastic fictions seen by the "eye of faith" need no further illustration. They are truly mind-boggling.

Of the many accounts which make clear the development of Mahayana beliefs resulting from a co-mingling with Hindu thought (in which one sees the "me-too" syndrome in the attempt to achieve the popular appeal of the traditional Hindu practices) a well-known exposition was given by A. K. Coomaraswamy. His "*Buddha and the Gospel of Buddhism*" was first published in 1916, but is now available in an updated version as a Harper Torchbook. Apart from a well-informed presentation of Mahayana thought in relation to Hinduism, it contains many charming versions of Buddhist lore which are usually embroidered from any original sober source with picturesque touches of magic: most appealing to a fancy-free mind. Much might be quoted from it but it will, perhaps, suffice to note: "We may remark here an important distinction between the Mahayana and the Hinayana (i.e., the Theravada) lies in the fact that the *former* is essentially mythical and unhistorical; the believer is, indeed, warned — precisely as the worshipper of Krishna is warned in the Vaishnava scriptures, that Krishna Lila is not a history, but a process for ever unfolded in the heart of man — that matters of historical fact are without religious significance."

Coomaraswamy's considered comment is that of a learned

brahmin. It strikingly illustrates the relation of the Mahayana to Hinduism, and it expresses a profound aspect of the purely religious outlook so especially characteristic of Hinduism: "matters of historical fact are without religious significance". It would be a notable gain if this comment were inscribed above the entry to all Hindu, Mahayana, and many other religious temples.

It is only reasonble for me to offer some positive appreciation of the Mahayana schools. This comes best from a devotee. Dr. Stcherbatsky has written: "When we see an atheistic, soul-denying, philosophic teaching of a path of personal final deliverance, consisting in an absolute extinction of life and a simple worship of the memory of its human founder — when we see it superseded by a magnificent High Church with a supreme God, surrounded by a numerous pantheon and a host of saints, a religion highly devotional, highly ceremonious and clerical, with an ideal of universal salvation of all living creatures, a salvation by the divine grace of Buddhas and Bodhisattvas, a salvation not in annihilation but in eternal life — we are fully justified in maintaining the history of religion has scarcely witnessed such a break." This could all be true in the context of religion, but it only serves to clarify that Theravada Buddhism is a philosophy.

A major motive leading to the differentiation of the Mahayana was the aim to promote the salvation of all living things. In pursuing this aim, Gotama was invested with a divine nature (all suggestions of which he himself appears to have strenuously denied) and this divinity was then sub-divided to produce several distinct deities, each with its special role. These imaginatively created figures provide appropriate foci for "special interest" worship. The further proliferation of bodhisattvas (that is, beings devoted to the salvation of others and themselves destined to become Buddhas) provides the generous help and, ultimately, "salvation" which the Mahayana sects offer. They incorporate an enormous body of mostly benevolent intentions, with incantations, formulae and recondite prescriptions of worship, charms and spells to sustain the faith of the devotees and to propel each one forward to a state of deliverance from earthly ties, that is, to the status of a bodhisattva.

There is an answer to the query, why indulge in such

elaborate, unrestrained fictional characterization? It is done deliberately to accommodate to, if not to compete with, the mythology of Hinduism. Its purpose is to take the compassion of the Buddha to the lay person. The goal is to achieve the six perfections: the perfections of giving, patience, morality, vigour, meditation and wisdom. But then Conze makes it brutally clear: "In actual fact there are no [multiple] Buddhas, no Bodhisattvas, no perfections and no stages. All these are products of our imagination, just expedients, concessions to the needs of ignorant people, designed to ferry them across to the Beyond." This might be called the higher, or rather, the lowest, duplicity. How could one get farther from the teacher who insisted, "Come and see"? Finally, however, all is resolved by the conclusion that "all is void": opposites are identical, yes is no. Solipsism takes over.

The doctrine of the void is an important element in Mahayana metaphysics. This thesis is approached from various directions. Gotama is quoted (with all good reason) as denying that he or any Buddha can be identified by specific physical marks, in fact that he had no such marks (e. g. the image of a wheel on his feet). In a masterstroke of fantasy, this is taken to indicate the non-perception of "ultimate" things. Alternatively, there is an interdependence of things, such as of fire on fuel. This is taken to "prove" that individual things have no substantial existence in themselves: the void is the true reality. This dismissal of the directly observed leads to "the world of wisdom and inconceivability, where the restrictions of our mind are removed". We are asked to remember that the actual world of interdependent causation becomes the void through the identity of affirmation and negation. (How this may be related to Orwell's "Yes is No" in 1984, I shall leave the reader to decide).

By thus insisting on the meaningless use of words, one passes immediately into the states of higher mysticism and one can remain permanently in nonsense-land. I apologise to the reader for presenting even this very brief abstract of what is an extensively developed mumbo-jumbo.

The flight from reason in these later schools of Buddhism almost certainly arose from the Brahminical-Hindu pressures and criticism. The doctrine of the void, which is specifically a Mahayana feature, can be ascribed to a perception of the limitations in language. Whilst the names for things remain constant, the things themselves frequently change. Especially so in the living world, where a playful young fox becomes a determined marauder. The acceptance of such variable or restricted meanings of words when pushed to extremes arrives at the conclusion that 'yes' is 'no' and 'black' is 'white". The paradoxes which can arise in this context were well known to some Greek philosophers, and they occupy their followers down to the present day.

The Tantric form of Buddhism found in Nepal and Tibet is described as a fusion of Mahayana doctrine with the indigenous belief in magical and necromatic ritual (Bön-po). It has been excused as a popular means of leading the uneducated layperson to an experience of "the void". One should probably accept that it provides a benign discipline and pleasurable rituals in which countless generations have found comfort. Intellectually it is as far from reason and the pragmatic truth as can be found outside mental hospitals.

In several of these sects not only is magic a prominent element, as in Taoism, but "religious" significance is given to the facts and practice of sex. Specific bodhisattvas have been created imaginatively to provide justification for ritual performances.

The extraordinary fact is that these patterns of belief have developed from "free association" with the calm, clear-headed teaching of Siddhattha Gotama. It is the transformation of a reasoned philosophy to over-heated religious fantasy.

It is appropriate here to make very brief indications of other forms into which Buddhism has been transformed.

Zen Buddhism

What we know as Zen Buddhism may be described as a mystically orientated Mahayana school. Originating in India, it was taken to China (*ca.* 520 A.D. by Bodidharma) where it greatly flourished, and was permanently influenced by Taoist mysticism. Having largely disappeared in China, Zen is now represented by Japanese sects, two of which are its principal expositors.

The emphasis is on self-knowledge and self-control. Mental states and mental appreciation are made all important. This leads to a mental acceptance of the equivalence of opposites, as these can be placed together in the mind. Faith and perseverance are essentials in the Zen pursuit of the Buddha nature. The individual is alone and must make his own way to enlightenment. Meditation is well known as the major element in Zen practice. But it is meditation "to empty one's mind", specifically of what are considered to be the illusions of the everyday world and of commonsense. Self-examination is emphasized. Values are created by the mind. Of these the greatest are truth, goodness, and beauty. The disciples of Zen are devoted to the cultivation of these values. All this was of great appeal to the finer elements in Japanese culture, where Buddhism had been strongly established from Chinese and Korean sources in the sixth-seventh centuries A.D. Although it is of a narrow content, it is truly Buddhist in the limited sense of its insistence that the individual must achieve enlightenment by his own effort.

Japanese sects

The Zen school, whilst more strongly represented in Japan than in any other country, is only a small part of the Buddhist scene in Japan. It is estimated that some thirty per cent of Japanese (i.e., some thirty million) are adherents of one or other of numerous Buddhist sects. The great majority of these are of essentially Mahayana character, each of the sects usually being particularly devoted to some single fictional element. These are worthy of notice perhaps only because they have, in total, played a dominant role in Japanese culture and especially in art: in poetry, painting, architecture, and landscape gardening, they have given Japan treasures of supreme human value.

One sect, Ritsu, derived from Theravada sources, has an ethical, disciplinary emphasis. It was taken to Japan at the emperor's invitation in the eighth century A.D., and is still active.

Purely Mahayana are the Sanron and Hosso sects. Derived from the writings of an Indian logician of the third century A.D., the former accepts a diluted version of the "all is void" thesis. Much studied by Japanese monks, this school is not committed to any formal doctrine, rather to sustained scepticism and a union of opposites. The Hosso are close to pure solipsism: nothing exists outside the mind.

Typical of many others is the Kegon sect. This is based on the supposed teachings of Buddha (Vairocana) first imagined in China. It emphasizes the unity of all things, the homogeneity of their forms and their interdependence. Worthy speculations these may well be, but it is difficult to see how this can in any way deserve the name Buddhist.

Related to Kegon and even more closely with themselves are the Tendai, Jodo and Nichiren sects. They give great prominence to the sutta (sermon) known as the Lotus of the True Law. This is the best known of all the innumerable Mahayana texts. In it the Buddha is a diety who works miracles: thus he shares only a complementary title with Siddhattha Gotama. All things are both void and transient, being both at once. These schools have a cosmology of heavens and hells, whose dominant characteistic is that of fantasty. Nevertheless, and probably thanks to their hugely imaginative features, these creations have played important roles in Japanese art.

The Jodo or Pure-Land (i.e., heavenly) sect is attached to a figure of great appeal: the Buddha of Infinite Light, a figure derived from a North Indian sutta of the second century A.D.: the Amida Buddha. Its devotees are committed to absolute faith in Amida Buddha from whom "salvation" is won by the reciting of his name and praises. Need it be said, it is very popular. Founded in Japan by Honen, this school has stimulated much music, dance, and drama (including the Noh plays), and the tea ceremony is associated with it.

The last of these related sects is that of Nichiren. He was a Japanese priest (1222-82) and a true missionary of his views. His teaching derives not from Gotama but from the Lotus Sutta. There is some emphasis on success in this world which has given it many converts, especially in this century which, consistent with the exclusively Japanese origin and development of the sect, has seen the elevation of Nichiren himself to the status of a Buddha worthy of worship.

These examples will serve to warn the reader — supposing he/she was otherwise unaware — of the extraordinary diversity, not to say aberration, to be found in that area of almost unlimited confusion and irrationality which is described as the Mahayana Buddhist religion.

Buddhism in Burma and in Sri Lanka

Practising Buddhists, in this country and abroad, will be aware that my account of Buddhism does not correspond to any of its observed forms. There are several reasons for this. Firstly, I have derided the conceptual basis of much of Mahayana Buddhism: and, of the more sober Theravada doctrine, I have rejected the belief in reincarnation (the cycle of birth-death-rebirth) and the undefinable concept of nibbana. Accordingly, what I have done is to attempt an exposition of those aspects of Theravada Buddhism — and they are many and hugely significant — which I find meaningful. Whatever the reader may make of this, he may well ask what is the character and practice of Buddhism in those communities where it has been long established?

This chapter is intended to provide some observations in that context.

My own experience of Buddhist communities has only been very cursory: in Sri Lanka, briefly in Burma, and more extended in two visits to Japan. Without adequate knowledge of the languages, my own evaluations could not be relied upon. However, there are, I would claim, excellent accounts by qualified observers which tell us much of what we wish to know in this respect.

Buddhism in Burma

For the Buddhist community in Burma I have chosen an account based on a careful field study made in the early 1960's by Professor M. E. Spiro of the University of California: *Buddhism and Society,* a volume of xix + 510 pages, with the subtitle, A great tradition and its Burmese viscissitudes, appeared in its second edition in 1982. It is an anthropological study of some considerable depth which affords many insights. I venture to offer a review of its appraisal of the Burmese scene.

Although one can claim that Buddhism is a unique doctrine, in many respects regarded as a religion — which is perhaps how many would now describe it in the Burmese community

— it shows the normal range of religious variability in both belief and practice. (The multiplicity of sects in Japan has already been mentioned.)

A major incursion of Theravada Buddhism into Burma took place in the eleventh century and the continuity of the tradition is shown by the staging of the 5th and 6th world councils of Buddhism in Burma in 1871 and 1954. The general pattern of its development shows the tendency to revert to beliefs and practices antecedent to Buddhism in Burma — a reversion to the national mythology — and to incorporate features of a pervasive Hindu character. Major consequences from the doctrine of impermanence (notably expressed in European thought by Goethe's: *Alles Vergänliches ist nur ein Gleichniss)* such as a qualified nihilism, a pessimism (as in Calvinism), and world-renunciation are very largely forgotten in daily life. One thinks of Johnson's friend who failed to achieve the status of a philosopher: "cheerfulness kept breaking in".

Spiro suggests that the great variations to be seen in the Buddhist's daily life in Burma can be (at least pragmatically) analysed in terms of three components: the aim to achieve nibbana: the operation of kamma: and what he names the "apo-tropaic" element — the desire, and the steps taken, to avoid the dangers, illness, and other threats to personal well-being in this life. Burmese Buddhists all show some degree of attachment to these three features, the third of which is in no clear sense Buddhist, but a return, both in concern and in practice, to pre-Buddhist behaviour patterns.

Despite the great differences between the bases of Christianity and Buddhism, Spiro avers, as an anthropologist, that in practice they are close to one another. Within each of the two separate communities there are ranges of opinion but, here, the Buddhist world is far more uniform than the Christian. The features marking the departure from basic Buddhist doctrine are principally those recognizable as infiltrations of Hindu practices, the acceptance of strictly non-Buddhist gods, spirits and indigenous rituals. Nevertheless, Burmese Buddhism is firmer in its forms and expressions than can be claimed for Buddhism even in Sri Lanka, Thailand, or Laos. Many accounts of the British period in Burma emphasized that the Burmese who are not Buddhists were regarded by the latter as non-Burmans. This view still tends to persist: from the village council to the national cabinet, non-Buddhists have traditionally not been fully accepted, nor are they readily trusted in positions of responsibility.

Throughout the Burmese countryside there is a widespread interest in all aspects of Buddhist teaching and practice: it is a constant concern of daily life. Observation shows that nibbana: kamma: the Buddha: metta: the sangha: etc., are recurring subjects for discussion amongst ordinary people. They are at least as frequent and as lively topics of conversation as the performance, weaknesses and strengths, of the local football team are in the English village pub. Much repetition of established opinions occurs, and particular prestige attaches to an ability to expound the basic aspects of Buddhist doctrine. In this context Spiro comments on one of the few dogmas in "this singularly undogmatic religion", that is the dogma of rebirth.

Some years ago a Burmese monk published a book in which he argued that in rebirth, humans would not, in his view, be reborn at a lower plane than the human. This was immediately labelled "a sacrilegious attack on Buddhism" and the All-Burma Abbots' Association voted to excommunicate the monk from the sangha.

Spiro reports a major clash between Buddhist principles and Burmese practice. This was seen "in defending the government policy of killing insurgents [in the north eastern provinces], executing criminals, granting licences for the slaughter of cattle and for distilling liquor. The Prime Minister, U Na, admitted that 'the Buddha would not like these [acts], and personally I would never be able to do them'. Still, sometimes it is necessary he argued, to perform undesirable acts to achieve some higher end, and he added 'there are many instances in the Jataka* tales to support this'." Despite this compromising stance of the government it is apparently only very rarely that a Burmese Buddhist will be found raising cattle, as they would eventually go to slaughter. The slaughterers are non-Buddhists, usually Muslims. Even the few Buddhist fishermen are

* The Jataka text is one of the major sources of Buddhist teaching. It has many accounts of Gotama's discourses and, specifically, has what is claimed to be his teaching on the problems of good government under the title "The ten duties of the king".

regarded with disdain. But naive casuistry was indulged in by the government when it introduced DDT insecticide for spraying in shops, homes, offices, etc. "The government does not kill the mosquitoes, it merely sprays the house: contact of the mosquitoes with the DDT is self-caused, so therefore is their death." That this simplicity was too thin a tissue was shown by the reluctance of nearly all Buddhists to assist in the use of DDT.

"Action, according to Buddhist teaching, is neither good nor bad except insofar as it is willful, intentional, purposive action. To lie unwittingly or to kill unintentionally is not accounted evil. As a discipline, this means Buddhism is principally concerned with the extinction of the desires which lead to immoral acts." (Spiro, loc.cit)

The Burmese Buddhists give the three major "impurities" as greed; hatred; and ingnorance. From the perspective of those seeking nibbana the guiding principle is not so much love as detachment. Love as an emotion is not highly regarded but three aspects of it, which are embraced in the concept of *metta*, are constantly emphasized as necessary parts of the Buddhist life. They are loving-kindness, a generalized and rational good-will and friendliness towards all living creatures: compassion or active sympathy for all who suffer: and the pleasure one should cultivate in sharing the happiness of others.

This benign outlook is encapsulated in the Burmese version of the metta-sutta, i.e., the creed of loving-kindness. As this may be described as the doctrine of the lay-buddhist's aims, it deserves quotation: idem. ibid., pp.269–270.

(i) Whatever is to be done by one who is skilful in seeking what is good, having attained that tranquil state of nibbana — let him be able and upright and conscientious and of soft speech, gentle, not proud.

(ii) And contented and easily supported and having few cares, unburdened, and with his senses calmed and wise, not arrogant, without showing greediness when going his round in families.

(iii) And let him not do anything mean for which others who are wise might reprove him; may all beings be happy and secure, and may they be happy-minded.

(iv) and (v) Whatever living beings there are . . . may all creatures be happy minded.

(vi) Let no one deceive another, let him not despise another in any place, let him not out of anger or resentment wish to harm another.

(vii) As a mother at the risk of her life watches over her own child, her only child, so also let everyone cultivate a boundless friendly mind towards all beings.

(viii) And let him cultivate goodwill to all the world, a boundless friendly mind, above and below and across, unobstructed, without hatred, without enmity.

(ix) Standing, walking, sitting, or lying, as long as he be awake, let him devote himself to his mind; this way of living, they say, is the best in this world.

(x) He who, not having embraced philosophical views, is virtuous, endowed with vision, after subduing greediness for sensual pleasures, will never again be reborn.

Spiro's extended account provides a thorough, deep assessment and analysis of Buddhism as practised in Burma. It is based on a careful and detailed observation of a rural community in which he lived. The day-to-day activities show a great attachment to Buddhist principles. These Spiro categorizes under the two headings of aiming for nibbana, and the acceptance of the operation of kamma. These both provide weighty emphasis supporting the metta-sutta. Much of the detail in village life corresponds closely with that reported by Gombrich for similar communities in Sri Lanka. Some of this is described later.

But in Burma, as the most casual visit reveals, the attachment to Buddhism is accompanied by a simultaneous belief in native spirits or local dieties. These are the *nats,* whose subsidiary but persistent role in the Burmese outlook is so fully accepted that shrines to them are often to be found within Buddhist temple grounds. A total of thirty-seven of these minor spirits have long been recognized: "minor" because their influence, which is often malevolent, is restricted in character and often localized to particular districts. Their possible evil intent has to be countered by charms, spells, ritual activity or gifts to their shrines. They appear to be accepted as existing quite apart from and at a subsidiary level to the Buddhist world where the law of kamma rules.

Spiro emphasizes that all this, truly extra-Buddhist element, provides a clear instance of the assimilation of primitive native spirit-worship into a higher superimposed philosophy or religion. Similar incursions or adhesions of native elements have occurred in most other countries where Buddhism has made entry, and often the more so the later the entry in the history of Buddhist diffusion. In Tibet, for instance, it might be wondered whether the native mythology has not retained the larger role in the amalgam with Buddhism.

Western observers very frequently form the impression that in a Buddhist temple the priests or lay members are to be seen praying, and even worshipping the Buddha image. Like so many others, Spiro provides the evidence to correct these major misconceptions. He relates how the first Anglican bishop in Rangoon, in 1877, put the question (through an interpreter) to a Buddhist monk who had long knelt in a prayerful posture: "For what and to whom are you praying?" Promptly, the reply came: "I am praying to nobody and for nothing". He was, of course, merely meditating on some aspects of the Buddha's teaching and of the path which he proffered. The main functions of the Buddha figure almost invariably found in a temple is to remind those attending of the character and guidance of Gotama. Few who have seen some of these evocative creations will deny they create an ambience in which the compassion and wisdom of the Tathagata comes to mind.

Spiro quotes (p.194) a Burmese monk: "Learned and sophisticated Buddhists can dispense with the Buddha statue completely, and concentrate instead on his teaching. The statue is only a crutch for ordinary people who require a visual symbol".

And a Burmese Buddhist layman: "The Buddha image is only a piece of wood like a doll. It is not to be worshipped. . . . People show respect to ordinary mortals. How much more should we pay respect to Buddha?"

How much indeed?

One major rent appears in the Buddhist flag which flies over Burma. The country contains a variety of different peoples and the north-east provinces, bordering on China, are still the sight of armed conflict with the Rangoon government. This is only the current state of much internal strife recorded in Burmese history. The dreadful feature of many dynastic changes, and even of royal successions within one family, was that a new incumbent in the throne felt obliged to stabilize his accession by having all potential challengers and their close relations slaughtered in what almost seems to have been a ritual process. This despite their total nominal adherence to Buddhism. Even some deviations occurred in the context of the most notable of the Buddhist dynasties. They were the kings, Anawrahta and his successors, whose capital was at Pagan, 150 kilometres south-west of Mandalay. There, in the royal succession (1044–1287), each aimed to outdo his predecessors in erecting beautiful Buddhist temples in the city which extended some eight kilometres along the banks of the Irrawaddy. Now largely, but not entirely in ruins, these temples, and the great number of stupas (ziggurat-like cenotaphs of all sizes), probably place Pagan only after Ankgor Vat and Borobudur in the heirarchy of major Buddhist monuments. The name Pagan has the same Sanskrit root as our English noun and means, in both cases, essentially "in or of the countryside".

Buddhism in Sri Lanka

The important role of Sri Lanka in the history of Buddhism has already been mentioned, and especially in the establishment of the Pali canon of the Theravada school as a result of the successful missions of Asoka's son, Mahinda, *ca.* 250 B.C. I shall make no attempt even to sketch the troubled history and fluctuating status of Sri Lankan Buddhism through later centuries. It is, however, relevant to mention that it was almost extinguished on at least two occasions when Tamil kings, who were Hindus, dominated the island. It is thus a sad fact that the outbreak in recent years of violence between Tamils and Sri Lankans has a longer history and a similar background to the situation in Ireland.

Our concern is the pattern of Buddhism in the normally peaceful central and southern provinces of Sri Lanka. Thanks to the even longer British regime in Sri Lanka than in Burma, English scholars and administrators have, for a century, written accounts of the Buddhist community in the island. I propose to base my summary on the extended account and analysis of Dr Richard Gombrich which first appeared as a Ph.D. thesis of Oxford University in 1968.

In the early '60s when Gombrich's field study was undertaken, of the total island population of ten and a half million, approximately seven and a half million were Sri Lankans (the remainder mostly Tamils and Hindus), of whom seven million were Buddhists and a half million Catholics — converts of the Portugese. The Buddhist community was led by seventeen thousand monks, divided into a number of sects.

It is of great value in Gombrich's work and writing that he is not committed to any pre-conceptions as to the character of Buddhism in practice. He quickly concludes that the Sri Lankan Buddhists, although their intellectual leaders are steeped in and are usually fully committed to the Theravada tradition, as lay persons they behave as though Buddha were a supernatural being. This means that their Buddhism has the character of a religion. Whilst this could be said to be generally true of the Mahayana sects, it is an interesting divergence between theory and practice to find most Sri Lankan Buddhists in the same category.* The Pali canon is quite explicit that Gotama insisted that he was no more than a teacher; and certainly was not to be worshipped.

A full exposition of Buddhist teaching was achieved by Buddhaghosa, the great commentator of the fifth century A.D. To a very large degree Buddhism, as actually expressed in Sri Lankan village life, is still distinctly canonical: it has changed little in fifteen hundred years. The major deviations — and there are several — amount to accretions, almost invariably from Hindu sources, of beliefs or practices not themselves part of the Buddhist canon. The belief in gods and demons (cf. the Burmese *nats*) at whose shrines offerings may be made by Buddhist laypersons is not regarded as a serious divergence. A monk is quoted as saying: "Gods are nothing to do with religion". As in Burma these subsidiary genii are regarded as a part of nature, and the simple-minded countryman calmly accepts them. Gombrich offers a telling comment: "An ordinary Buddhist layman is no more concerned to accept or deny some new supernatural being than a Western layman is concerned to accept or deny the existence of some newly

* Appropriately, Gombrich quotes Spiro: "Religion is an institution consisting of culturally patterned interaction with culturally postulated [i.e., supposed or actual historic] superhuman beings." Note that Gombrich can describe Sri Lankan Theravadins as "religious" for two reasons: the lay people accept that description, and, also, they do frequently incorporate local spirits or deities into their traditions, But the teaching of the Tathagata is essentially a close-to-rational philosophy, whatever its adherents may themselves add to its content.

discovered type of nuclear particle." One can imagine that the evidence for the supernatual spirits may appear to be more direct and convincing than is that for the neutrino to most readers of the daily press. Whilst he did not involve them in his teaching, there is good reason to suggest that Gotama himself accepted the existence of spirits which were certainly a fully accredited part of his Hindu world.

When the government issued a text for the early teaching of Buddhism in schools it contained the indication that Buddhism was not so much a religion as a way of life. Despite this being entirely consonant with pure Theravada doctrine, it produced a storm of protest, much of it claiming that Marxism had infiltrated the Department of Culture.

There is at least a small temple in nearly every village. Apart from a few simple ceremonies performed by the monks (especially on days associated with the Buddha's birth, enlightenment, and death), there are no established rituals for the lay Buddhist. The temple is a place for meditation or for hearing readings or recitings by the monks. The Tathagata is dead: he cannot hear prayers or aid suppliants but much merit is gained by showing respect as by placing flowers picked in the fields or woods at Buddha's image. The action is accompanied by reciting two Pali verses:

> "This heap of flowers which has colour and
> scent I offer at the blessed lotus feet of
> the lord of sages."
>
> "I make offering with these flowers and by
> this merit may there be release [from the
> trials of this world?]. Just as these
> flowers fade, so my body goes towards destruction."

Similar traditional verses are used by the simplest laypersons in offerings of incense, lamps, or scarves. The merit is in the intention of paying respect to the Buddha. It is, apparently, an incursion from Hindu practice to offer food at a Buddha image: the original meaning in this case was that of sustaining the god or his priests.

Some simple ceremonies regularly performed at village temples, when some play-acting and reading is done to the accompaniment of drumming and playing of instruments, are occasions for fund collecting for the temple. The form of such ceremonies is often long in tradition, being derived from acts of tribute to the early kings of Sri Lanka and now transferred to the Buddha.

Another "conservation of practice" is seen in the credence given to horoscopes, even by monks or those entering the priesthood. The dominance of the Hindu world is explicit in this case, as it is accepted that Gotama condemned astrology, palmistry, and similar practices, declaring them to be irrelevant distractions and unhelpful on the path to nibbana. Many lay Buddhists, in town and country, visit the shrines of local deities. Incantations and spells are uttered with intent to gain some advantage which is promoted by money or gifts left at the shrine. Gombrich comments, however, that most of those indulging in such practices are aware of the flimsy bases for their actions, much as those visiting the palmist at a U.K. fair. It forms a relief from the burdens of daily life.

Living in a remote village for the better part of a year allowed Gombrich to be accepted as a member of the community in which he learned the self-expressed views of the villagers and he could, after some time, discreetly question them with some confidence, further to establish their own opinions. Although the extent of their knowledge was often only very slight, their expressed beliefs were still surprisingly close to the teaching of the early Pali canon. That their actions frequently diverged from it led Gombrich to wonder whether that had not always been so. It must, however, be remembered that periods of Tamil-Hindu and more recently European (Portugese, Dutch, and British, in that order) domination have injected prolonged intervals of disturbance in the Sri Lankan scene. It would have been amazing if the natives had retained a culturally pure pattern of behaviour.

As in Burma, the attainment of nibbana has receded from practical concern, even for the monks who accept that no recent examples of its achievement can be quoted. Meditation likewise, is practised only by few, mostly elderly Buddhists. The over-riding concern is with morality — the five precepts and the ten good deeds — and the aim is to build up merit so as to ensure a good rebirth. The canonical theory of kamma appears to have survived intact and has a dominant role in guiding behaviour.

In those districts where poorer natives indulge in hunting to make up their food supplies, it is immediately recognized that much negative merit is thus generated. The aim then is to cancel this by conscious effort — by helping others, showing respect, rejoicing in another's merit, and self-control. Generosity to strangers is constantly exhibited throughout the Buddhist community. In country villages "it borders on the incredible".

Apart from those of a Mahayana persuasion (and a minority of Sri Lankan Buddhists are in that category) all agree that there is no external help for the aspiring Buddhist. Each individual must develop his/her own internal strengths. There is no-one to pray to.

Again, the role of intention is of the greatest importance and this is accepted in the assessment of individuals' behaviour. Greed, passion, hatred and delusion are universally condemned. (Television had clearly not arrived). Bad behaviour is often ascribed to stupidity which, in turn, is accepted as a part of human experience. Anyone leaving valuables where they can be stolen is guilty of stupidity and is condemned for exposing people to temptation. Despite general rational censure there is much thieving and, by Buddhist standards, very unacceptable levels of homicide and adultery.

Vegetarianism is practised by only a minority of Sri Lankan Buddhists: it is greatly approved of and occasionally, the villagers in the country will boycott the (Muslim) butcher's shop to establish at least a temporary disapproval.

The most striking evidence of an irresistible Hindu influence on the Buddhist community in Sri Lanka is the presence of caste divisions. There are very many fewer castes than in India: some two dozen in all, defined essentially by the means of livelihood. In the central hilly country there are only about half a dozen castes. The differences between the castes are not pronounced and, in public, the visitor is very rarely aware of their existence.

It is probably true to say that Gotama accepted caste as a feature of life in his environment and he made no special drive against it. He did, undoubtedly, emphasize that entry into the community he was intent on establishing was completely independent of caste, which was entirely irrelevant and, indeed, contrary to his tenets. The Sri Lankan monks are fully conscious of this and express shame at a situation which, they explain, was forced on them in earlier times. There is much social interchange between the various castes, except those furthest apart: at socials, food and drink is exchanged by all, but there is little marriage outside one's own caste and there are differences in manner of speech. Much of this pattern of behaviour is, of course, found in communities with a strongly feudal background such as Japan and nearer to home.

What is particularly distasteful is the fact that of three major groups of Buddhist temples in Sri Lanka, entry to two of them is more readily achieved if not fully restricted to members of the higher castes. Centralized organizations of each group has ensured that an accepted pattern is maintained. The one group which pays no attention to caste has, not surprisingly, a tradition of political activity and of reform, further to eliminate all traces of caste.

Many of the departures from the still well-recognized doctrine of Theravada Buddhism in Sri Lanka have resulted from interference by rulers and from the abandonment of the wandering life of early converts who kept in contact with all members of the community. In the monasteries, the emphasis has been on learning and in preservation and exposition of the early doctrine. This has isolated the monks and given them, in Sri Lanka, an element of un-Buddhist superiority. The female branch of the Sangha has also long disappeared from the island.

Despite its important role in the early history of Buddhism and its retention of a largely pure Theravada doctrine, the state of Buddhism practised in Sri Lanka is clearly of a mixed and diluted character.

A final comment on Buddhism in Sri Lanka, is culled from a different source. Dr. Carrithers made a direct, personal field study of the community of monks living in the forested areas of central Sri Lanka. I quote from his summary (p.77): "Many were tranquil, healthy and contented, to be sure, but three features of their behaviour and attitudes stood out as being directly attributable to their training. The first was an interested, indeed fascinated, absorption in what they called their 'work' — (i.e., their daily round of activities, duties, meditation, etc.) . . . The second trait is linked to the first: they did nevertheless pour energy and years of their lives into long-term projects, such as the founding of forest hermitages, but many evinced in attitude and in action a marked lack of anxiety about the future of their efforts. . . . But the most vivid trait was the third, the monks' calm courage in the face not only of physical infirmity, but also of the sudden danger from animals which lived in the forest with the monks. It was this which, to my mind, attested to the depth of transformation achievable through the Buddhist training. None of this, of course, proves the truth of the Buddha's teaching, but it does invite us to consider his philosophy seriously as one which even today has something to tell us about the nature and capacities of the human constitution".

In recent years, and especially in Sri Lanka, there has been an increasing incursion of Buddhist monks into politics, usually from a liberal, socialist, or Marxist position. This is in no way a feature peculiar to Buddhism. It is occuring very extensively and perhaps most intensively in the Roman Catholic priesthood, especially in South America. But whether for good or for ill, no-one can claim that such intervention has its roots in the Tathagata's teachings.

Buddhist Art

Let me say that I can only draw attention to some aspects of Buddhist Art. For an adequate account some of the many volumes by specialists in this area must be consulted.

Theravada Buddhism was firmly focused on the individual and his detachment from the trials and temptations of this world. It expressly forbade "the low arts of divination, spells, omens, astrology, sacrifices to gods, witchcraft and quackery". These were the constant features of the Brahminical world. In dismissing them the early Theravadins appear also to have restricted the fine arts and to have excluded fanciful decoration and even representation of the human form. This last prohibition would also have arisen from the insistence that the Tathagata was in no way to be worshipped, a prohibition which still stands. Accordingly, it is to the Mahayanists that we owe the major creations in Buddhist art and all credit must be accorded them for their great achievements.

It is historically interesting that the earliest images of Gotama were produced in North-west India in the Kingdom of Gandhara (now Peshawar). This was far from Gotama's home in north-east India. Around the first century A.D. Greek influences (not that of Alexander the Great who died 323 B.C.) led to the depiction of the Buddha in human form. Previously, whilst there were many works depicting aspects or incidents associated with Buddhist teaching, Gotama was represented only in symbolic forms, by the wheel, the lotus, or his footprints, etc. The early Gandhara figures show the most obvious Hellenic character: whilst the heads are Indian, the hair, the shoes, the drapery, etc., are often almost purely Greek. We must remember that out of the petty Greek principalities around Kabul (Afghanistan) there emerged the Greek ruler Menander, who conquered large areas in the Punjab and in the Ganges valley. It was he who was converted to Buddhism by Nagasena, to whom are owed the Milinda (i.e., Menander) suttas.

It is thus possible that the traditional image of Gotama so widely diffused through east Asia owes much to Greece. But the Buddhist artists must be given the credit for creating so many extremely convincing and subtle presentations of the calm serenity, majestic enlightenment, and sublime compassion to be found in the Buddha figures.

Buddhist temples reflect a different aim from churches or mosques. They are not so much intended for formal occasions as the public worship of the Christian and Moslem worlds. Their aim is more limited: to create an ambience and environment in which the visitor is reminded of the character of the Tathagata, his teaching, and the peace which it provides. Nothing in or around the temple belongs to another world: there is no mystery of holy-of-holies: but always much genuine respect is given to Buddha statues, shrines or stupas. There are no tombs of kings, princes, field-marshals, or admirals. Wordly office conveys no status in Buddhism.

As the temple belongs to this world, its surroundings can be as important as its contents. Especially is this true of many examples in Japan. In Kyoto, Kinkakuji (the Golden Temple) is a small wooden pavilion at the edge of a small water-scape, in which rocks are located with the art which conceals art: but the extensive grounds of many acres have a variety, including a large hill-side of planted trees, and a lake of the Chinese ducks, offering a range of 'natural' views whose contrivance represents an artistic masterpiece. On a first visit, my experience was of having chosen, from the many hundred temples described in Kyoto and near-by Nara, a list of seventeen to be viewed in five days: only by determined efforts at detachment did I succeed in visiting eleven. Having climbed up to Kyo-mitsu via Tea-pot Lane, it was peculiarly difficult to leave after many hours.

Even this cursory note on Buddhist monuments cannot omit a reference to at least some of its best known instances. At Borobodur, in central Java, there is a low hill cased in a pyramidal shell of intricately carved stone. The sculptured reliefs cover the successive terraces which are traversed as one ascends from one level to the next to a total length of some three kilometres. The seven terraces depict hundreds of stories from Mahayana literature, a multitude of small stupas carry statues of the Buddha, and the whole is crowned by a great stuppa or relic shrine, a form of cenotaph used in Buddhist monuments although originating in Vedic sources. The whole structure is a representation in stone of many aspects of Mahayana mythology. Recently restored by international effort over several years through the offices of the United Nations, it has been called "the most magnificent achievement of Indian art", as it is the culture and craftsmanship of northern India which is there preserved.

In a similar category are the Ajanta caves (some 350 km north east of Bombay) with their sculptures and paintings: the earliest of the latter date from *ca.* 100 A.D. It was the Khmer rulers in Cambodia (now Kampuchia) who built Angkor Thom ("the great town") as their capital, firstly *ca.* 900 A.D. That city itself has many Hindu-Buddhist temples, the two traditions being almost inseparably mixed. It was *ca.* 1140 A.D. that the greatest achievement of Khmer architecture, the great temple complex of Angkor Wat, ("the temple town") approximately a square of one kilometre sides, was constructed on a site outside the city proper. Whilst many Hindu features were incorporated, Angkor Wat was dedicated to Mahayana Buddhism.

More strictly a monument to Buddhist culture — and in the Theravada tradition — is the ruined site of Pagan in Burma. An extensive city along the bank of the Irrawaddy river, it was the capital of Upper Burma for over two hundred years, until it was over-run by Kublai Khan in 1287. "Pagan is in many respects the most remarkable religious city in the world.

Jerusalem, Rome, Kiev, Benares, none of these can boast the multitude of temples, and the lavishness of design and ornament that make marvellous the deserted capital on the Irrawaddy ... the whole space is thickly studded with pagodas of all sizes and shapes, and the very ground is so thickly covered with crumbling remnants of vanished shrines, that according to the popular saying you cannot move a foot or hand without touching a sacred thing." (Sir James Scott, *The Burman, his life and notions*: 1881). Suffice it to mention only two items at Pagan, the Ananda temple and the Shwezigon pagoda, and to say (with a very unBuddhist lack of modesty) that each of them, as a work of art, is in the same category as the cathedral at Chartres.

Of other aspects of Buddhist art I would only remind the reader that the richness of Japanese art owes a very great deal to Buddhist — albeit Mahayana — sources. The first stages of classical Japanese culture developed with the introduction of Buddhism from the sixth century onwards. Not only missionaries but artists and craftsmen came from China and Korea. Their gifts were of supreme quality. Two examples only: the Ho-o-do (ie.e the Phoenix building) temple at Uji, near Kyoto, was built in Chinese style firstly as a princely palace, but was soon converted to a Buddhist temple. Modest in size, and so entirely human in conception, it is of a perfection rare in any art. Then, amongst the numerous treasures at Horiuji is the life-size wodden sculpture of the Matreyia Buddha (i.e. the Buddha-to-come), ascribed to the prince, monk, and artist Shitoku. That this exquisite masterpiece was not the product of sudden inspiration is proved by several of its fore-runners, in the attempt to capture the ineffable, which are to seen in the National Museum at Seoul.

Another well-known item in Japanese culture in which the Buddhist influence is established is the poetic verse known as haiku. This developed — in fact, became detached from — a traditional pattern of poetry in which the opening had a sequence of five, seven, and five syllables. These seventeen syllables are the gnomic form, haiku. Matsuo Basho (1644-94) was the master who raised this simplest of forms to be a universally appreciated and, at the same time, frequently a subtle, highly cultivated poetic element which still retains great popularity in Japan. Basho was of a samurai family. He led a wandering life, at one time intending to enter a Buddhist monastery, but he remained a traveller-poet. Several of his disciples were even closer to Buddhism than Basho, whose works carry the smile of a man who has transcended suffering.

It is perhaps impossible briefly to convey the atmospheric quality of the best haiku. There are many aspects of Japanese thought, apart from Buddhist elements, carried by these simple lines. A typical comment is made by H. G. Henderson in his *Introduction to Haiku* (Doubleday Anchor Books, New York, 1958): "... one might wonder whether the poet really put into it all the deep meaning that one finds. But the proof is overwhelming that ... Basho did put into most if not all his later haiku all the meaning that anyone can find, and probably much more." (Much of the justification for this comes from observations which Basho himself, or his attendant pupils, made of the compositions.) "Among the qualities which are often considered as indicative of (Basho's attachment to) Zen are a great zest for life; a desire to use every instant to the uttermost: an appreciation of this even in natural objects; a feeling that nothing is alone, nothing unimportant, and an acute awareness of relationships of all kinds ...".

Numerous other writers of haiku show Buddhist influences in their sharp insistence on the beauty of the simplest things in nature, the appeal of those things which bend with or are indifferent to the strains and stresses of life. Slender, fragile and humble things are constantly verse subjects: the warrior, the fierce tiger, the powerful lord never appear. "Basho has no less love for the humblest things of nature than for humanity: all are part of one vast whole and intermingle, but are never — as in Wordsworth — the manifestation of a Supreme Being."* The genius of haiku is the expression of an emotion as one indivisible whole, the momentary essence of which can only be achieved by the immediate appreciation of a few significant words. This aim, to convey by apparently simple means, the nuance of a situation or the ambience of a place, is a guiding theme throughout Japanese art.

A Japanese scholar would certainly choose examples which carry telling, if subtle, references to traditional stories or

* *Haikai and Haiku,* published by the Japanese Classics Translation Committee (Nippon Gakujutsu Shinkokai), Tokyo, 1958. The examples of haiku have been taken from this volume.

historic events. The following examples require no explanatory comments: the romanized Japanese is given in some cases.

Kiku no ka ya / Nara ni wa furuki / hotoke-tachi
The scent of chrysanthemums! At Nara are ancient images of Buddhas.

(Basho, 1644–94)

Grasping at nothing, the frog by itself floats on the water.
(Joso, 1662–1704)

Furu-sato mo / ima wa karine ya / watari-dori.
Birds of passage! I, too, am a bird of passage in my native village.

(Kyorai, 1651–1704)

Kare-ashi no / hini-hini orete / nagarekeri.
Broken reeds day by day float away.

(Ranko, 1726–98)

Ato-zama ni / ko-u-o naga-ruru / shimizu kana.
See the little fish swim back against the stream.
(Kito, 1741–89)

What dreams is the butterfly dreaming that she flutters her wings?

(Chiyo-jo, 1703–75)

Evening swallow! For me, no counting on the morrow.
(Issa, 1763–1827)

Please, stay your hand; the fly is rubbing its hands and its feet.
(Issa)

The world is dew, the world is dew, and yet . . .

(Issa)

Even shorter than the haiku is the seven/seven sylable *wakiku*. Here Basho produced:

Hito-fuki kaze no / ko-no-ha shizumaru.
A puff of wind; then the leaves lie still.

5
Conclusions

In this chapter I hope to summarize briefly some of the details of earlier sections and to offer comments on the position facing Buddhist teaching in the late twentieth century world.

Historical Status

The early Pali and Sanskrit sources are in over-all accord. It is not clear which can establish precedence, but the Pali sources appear the more complete and, in some sense, their account is more systematically presented. Both are much contaminated by fictional embellishment and a variety of magical elements. In view of the lapse of at least three centuries from Gotama's death to the earliest known occasion when the teaching was committed to record, the accretion of supernatural detail cannot be taken to discredit the whole of the accounts. No disciples of a prominent teacher of the sixth century B.C. in northern India could resist the temptation of adding celestial detail to their records.

Very difficult, if not impossible, is the task of deciding how close the magic-shorn record approaches historic fact. Much plausible detail — such as the account of Gotama's leaving home with his favourite steed and charioteer — is very probably colourful expansion of what was originally simple incident. All such narrative can be discarded, except insofar as one wishes to establish the personal aura of Siddhattha Gotama.

Of the historical reality of the teacher there can be only minimal doubt. All the significant sources, apart from agreeing on a substantial core, are composed of a huge variety of items. In all these, the presence of a single, totally consistent persona is indelibly inscribed.

This character is of a piece with that captured by many of the early representations of Buddha, although these only came four or more centuries after his death, and can in no way be taken to approach an accurate physical likeness. Like so many thousands of later modellings, they merely represent the artist's version of what had become a firmly established tradition. They are the artist's creation of a figure to match the impressions carried by reading the Buddhist canon.

The most significant question of historicity is — to what degree do we have a valid account of Gotama's own discourses? The answer cannot be more than conjecture. Accepting, what is inescapable, that he was a truly remarkable teacher, each student will make his own choice of what he would advance as close to authentic material.

E. J. Thomas was a principal historian of Buddhism. He refers to the congregation of disciples which, almost certainly, occurred at the Buddha's death. There is no significant surviving evidence for what occurred at that time and so the title of First Buddhist Council is perhaps inappropriate. But Thomas concludes;* "At the time of Buddha's death there must have been many discourses which the disciples knew by heart and we need not doubt that they were collected and recited in a 'chanting together or *sangita*.'" Many of the discourses have such a brilliantly simple didactic character, with an element of calm irresistible common sense, that, at least, they have originated from a teacher of genius. It is the content of the discourses which eventually is all that is significant today; the value of the philosophy which emerges is quite independent of any questions of personal origin. The poetry of Homer is by no little devalued because of uncertainties of authorship.

The early records provide quite the minimum of uncertainty that the teaching of Gotama was in no way a religion (there being nothing to worship), and not even metaphysical, but rather a down-to-earth appraisal of the human predicament with a plan for minimizing its distresses.

One of the supreme virtues which can be claimed for the

* E. J. Thomas, *History of Buddhist Thought*, Routledge and Kegan Paul, London, 1951.

Tathagata is his insistence that each of those interested in his outlook should accept nothing of which he was not convinced. Probably the first, he is certainly the greatest of teachers to have emphasized such a discrimination. It is the ultimate indication of the confidence this teacher had that he had arrived at the truth. And it allows his disciples, outside established sects, to make their own evaluation of his teaching and to accept what they find is valid. Certainly that is what I am engaged in doing.

The Teaching: nine aspects

No two students would make the same selection of those items they most value in the teaching ascribed to Gotama. The following is merely my own list.

(i) The emphasis on truth, a criterion not elevated to some abstract or absolute form, but essentially pragmatic.

With a clear denial of the absolute, all "truth" can be accepted only insofar as it survives extended experience.

(ii) The denial of the supernatural.

The early records leave little doubt that Gotama rejected all aid, communication, and knowledge of beings from another "plane of existence", such as quasi-heavenly bodhisattvas. In any case, we can be confident of the fantasy in such details.

Most important — because of its decisive significance — is Gotama's denial of any knowledge of a Supreme Being or of a soul.

Here his insight and courage in clinging to the real world is exemplary. By their own acceptance that a super-natural element is involved, all those claiming reality for these mental constructs are giving material weight to what does not belong in this world. Once the unknowable is admitted to "reality" there can be no limit to deception.

The freedom from illusion provided by this stance is one large element in Buddhist enlightenment.

(iii) Cognate to the preceding thesis — one might perhaps claim it as its generalization — is the emphasis on ignorance as the root of so many human problems. Here Gotama is by no means alone, but he is the first of the philosophers to elevate this view to the status of a general principle.

(iv) Toleration has been an invariable characteristic of Buddhist teaching. It is well illustrated in several instances of

Gotama's exchanges with those of other views and even with aggressive challengers.

Allowing freedom of thought and freedom of attachment to other beliefs proves to be an essential for any advancement in civilization. Those denying these freedoms are putting the human mind in chains.

(v) Respect for life in all its forms. This is an extension of the principle of human tolerance to the rest of the natural world.

In this insistence, Gotama was not the first. There was already the doctrine of *ahimsa* in the Indian world: i.e., respect for and protection of all forms of life. Mahavira, the greatest of the Jain teachers, and Gotama's contemporary, raised this teaching to a supreme status.

The Buddhist stance avoids an absolutist position. Life must not, without provocation, be threatened or taken. There is no prohibition to defending oneself if attacked. It is all-important to emphasize that the Buddhist, having no intention of attacking others, will not prepare to do so. He will positively avoid any suggestion of threatening another. This means that Buddhists are pacifists. And, in some degree, they have been vegetarians and conservationists for more that two thousand years before these attitudes became popular in Europe.

(vi) The eight-fold path provides a strictly defined pattern of high moral purpose.

Many readers will feel this aspect should be given a higher place in this summary. Its location in this list in no way reflects any qualification of its value. The delay in referring to it reflects the fact that high moral standards have been enjoined by all worthy teachers.

It can be claimed for the Tathagata that he was the first to spell out clearly, and in a fully detailed way, the behaviour pattern commensurate with the highest ideals. He ennumerates the essential and practical steps which can ensure that the individual both attains and maintains an irreproachable character.

As applied to the order of the monks the basic rules of conduct are ten.

1. Never destroy life.
2. Never take what is not offered.
3. Never engage in sexual relations.

4. Never lie nor engage in harmful talk.
5. Never take intoxicants or drugs.
6. Do not eat between meals.
7. Avoid secular entertainments.
8. Avoid scents, jewelry, and personal adornment.
9. Avoid luxurious beds or chairs or an excessive concern for comfort.
10. Avoid money transactions.

Of these direct rules, the layman is expected to obey the first five, and then the third is interpreted as a strict injunction against adultery.*

(vii) Consistent with, if not in fact immediately allied to the earlier principles, Buddhist teaching is completely clear as to the unity of the world.

This means that such horrors as nationalist antagonisms and racism are entirely foreign to Buddhist precepts. I desist from any account of how these plagues have infected the European world. Confucius was only some ten years or so younger than Gotama, and not for the first time in this series of items, he agreed with the Tathagata. His well-known expression was: "He who respects the dignity of man, and practises what love and courtesy require — for him all men within the four seas are brothers."

The Tathagata had acquired, from brahminical cosmology, the conviction that other physical worlds than ours existed. Buddhist teaching (maybe developed by extension from the Tathagata's own indications) accepts that Buddhist enlightenment will prove equally illuminating in these other worlds. This suggestion can well be characterized as extremely fanciful: that must be granted. It is, however, a vast improvement on so many other outlooks, and specifically the Judaeo-Christian-Moslem view, as these religions regard this particular world of ours as uniquely significant in the universe. Let us acclaim the liberating extension of our horizon shown by Buddhism in denying any such supposed unique position of our minute world in the cosmos. Twenty-five centuries after its intuitive presentation, we now know it to be true.

---

* The bringing of a child into this world is, to a Buddhist, an undertaking of the very gravest order, and such irresponsibility as leads to single parent "families" can only be regarded as of criminal intent

(viii) The records show that Gotama repeatedly insisted that we must each find our own way towards enlightenment.

This is another instance of the great confidence the Tathagata had in his own teaching and in his fellow humans. He knew how much easier it would be if he were to present himself as a "saviour", simple reliance on whom would be adequate to survive the trials of this world. A number of teachers of that persuasion are extant even today. The Tathagata was not interested in easy solutions. He positively rejected attempts by his disciples to elevate him to some supra-normal plane. He favoured a genuine care for the world's ills which would not depend upon his presence. For this, individuals must acquire their own conviction that they, too, had themselves grasped the effective truth of the human situation. Then all could stand securely on their own feet.

Gotama made it very clear that no individual, no incantations, no rites, had any value to be compared with the dhamma — i.e, the teaching.

(ix) Compassion has always been credited as a major element in Gotama's character. It has likewise always been a major virtue in the Buddhist ethic. It might, in fact, be claimed as its foundation. "True wisdom consists not in metaphysical sophistication but in practical knowledge expressed in compassion as the fundamental principle in social life."

Sympathy, benevolence, charity and love for every living being are enjoined in all Buddhist teaching. Preceding sections have not elaborated on this ethic, as the principal concern has been to comment on the coherence and appeal of the Tathagata's teaching. The demand for good-will and its practical exercise must be given the major status accorded them by Gotama's disciples. Some of the most frequent injunctions can be quoted:

> "Refraining from error, doing good works,
> and purifying one's mind, this is the
> Buddhist doctrine."

> "One does not repay evil by evil, but
> one repays evil with good."

> "One should overcome anger through kindness,
> wickedness through goodness, selfishness
> through charity, and falsehood through truth."

Carrithers writes: "In the Buddhist texts compassion is analysed into three: first, compassion proper, defined as sympathy with others' suffering; second, sympathetic joy, the pleasure at another's good fortune; and third, loving-kindness, the Buddhist sentiment *par excellence.*"

Social Relations

Frequently emphasized in the Tathagata's discourses were the differences that must be expected, and are almost invariably found, between people from different backgrounds. The Buddhist is reminded that he must bear this in mind even in acts of charity. For this reason ample sensitivity is needed to secure what is highly desirable, that is, social cooperation and active public participation in good works. Only through such activity can the individual experience the bonds of common humanity. Everything that fosters these should be encouraged.

The differences between various Buddhist sects have already been emphasized. The sober, realist, undemonstrative character of, say, Sri Lankan Theravada practice, and the noisy, spirit-ridden orgiastic pattern of Tantric Buddhism are so far apart as almost to obliterate any common features. Yet neither of these groups would think of denouncing the other. They would both insist that every person must find his/her own way to enlightenment. Toleration has very deep roots in Buddhism. Wars of religion such as have occurred so frequently in Europe are inconceivable in Buddhism. The Spanish Inquisition of the horrors detailed in Motley's *Rise of the Dutch Republic* could only be nightmares to a Buddhist.

In past centuries differences in character could be seen in the charitable works undertaken by Buddhist monks in the Theravada and Mahayana disciplines. The principal motive leading to the expansions of the Mahayana school which took place in northern countries (Nepal, China, Mongolia, Japan, etc.) was that of enhancing contact between the monks and the lay people. This led to Buddhists being active and often instigating and developing benevolent public services: hospitals, homes for the aged, schools, improvements in roads, irrigation, etc. Theravada centres (Sri Lanka, Burma, Cambodia, etc.) were principally in countries where the basic requirements of food and shelter were usually readily available. This tended to limit the monks to more personal aspects of charity, that is, to families or individuals. It is also clear that the differentiation reflects the original emphasis in Theravada teaching on the need for the individual to achieve enlightenment by his/her own efforts.

Emphasis on the attainment of nibbana was certainly dominant throughout the monastic order in earlier centuries, and this may still be true in some higher circles of the Theravada world. The vast majority and specifically, it appears, lay-Buddhists, are satisfied with lower aims. Accepting the operation of kamma, the aim is to abide by the principles taught by Gotama and to achieve not only the satisfaction, stability, and peace-of-mind which are the certain rewards of a beneficent life-pattern, but also to establish the basis for life of enhanced enlightenment.

Relations to Christianity

Much of the early appreciation of Buddhism reached Europe via scholars with a background, if not a specific attachment, in Christian belief. This applied even well into the present century and led to occasional misrepresentations. In many cases what seems to have happened amounted to identification of features in Buddhist teaching with those in the Christian gospels. Unquestionably some such identifications were valid: even then it had to be remembered that insofar as the Buddhist sources were genuine, that teaching had historical priority of the order of six centuries. One systematic presentation of common features is to be found in an appendix in Carus's *The Gospel of Buddha*, Chicago, 1904. There is no need for me to pursue these details, but one can point out that the use of the term "gospel" already introduces an element foreign to Buddhism, in that it implies a message "from on High".

Readers of Walpole Rahula's "*What the Buddah Taught*" will find instances of how misconceptions have arisen through incorrect translations of Pali texts. Thomas, in his *Life of the Buddha*, tells us that the first Christian writer to mention Buddha was Clement of Alexandria at the end of the third century A.D. Clement writes of "those of the Indians that obey the precepts of Brutta, whom through exaggeration of his dignity they honour as a god". Later, St. Jerome in discussing virgin births instances Buddha as one who shared this distinction. These intended compliments — of being a god and having a virgin birth — would not have appealed to Gotama. Nor the frequent suggestion that he offers some form of "salvation". Even the majority of Mahayana schools do not indulge in such a claim. What the Tathagata taught was "one is one's own refuge".

The wish to find a truly Christian element in Buddhist teaching dies hard. I am in no way inclined to challenge this aim, nor am I capable of denying any success it may have, but I do find some attempts in this direction remarkable as instances of special pleading. In a very enlightened brief volume, *World Religions* (Watts and Co. Ltd., London, 1966), Professor H. D. Lewis gives an acceptably clear summary of the Buddhist position: e.g., on p.160: "Man finds his salvation in himself and for himself, there is no divine intervention, no mediation, no sublime object of worship outside of man himself." And then, (p.167) he quotes one statement in the Pali canon where the Tathagata appears to emphasize the limits of agnosticism and so, I quote, "We are not to say that we can say nothing; and this seems to me to give agnosticism a twist which completely alters its character and brings it into line with the acknowledgement of an ultimate mystery, a mystery whose ultimate and positive nature is discerned in a peculiarly incisive and modern way."

Notice that what is given a new interpretation is *agnosticism*, and that this is simultaneously being associated, if not identified, with Buddhism. How far this can capriciously be taken is seen on p.170 where we find that the Ultimate (or God) becomes "altogether elusive, He is 'wholly other' or 'beyond' in the most absolute mystery." To the best of my knowledge, at no stage whatever did Gotama allow a role for the transcendental in his essential message. A careful reading, even of the brief extracts quoted, suffices to show how anxiously a serious scholar can twist a comment of Gotama's to bring him into line with Christian mysticism.

The Historic Human Situation

In all the philosophical and religious discussions of our understanding of the human world, even in such apparently detached analyses as those of Bertrand Russell, there seems to me to be a major assumption for which I can find no justification. It is assumed that if we collect the facts observed and the experiences encountered in our human world, we can retire to our studies, systematize these findings, and then also make deductions about some "ultimate" content or principles which are behind and beyond the recorded evidence. Plato has been a key-figure in injecting this pre-occupation into western thought. For a period of over two thousand years the results have usually been, and still are, disastrous. They lead to a detachment from the real world and the assumption of knowledge (which often becomes dogma) from a superior, unseen world. Although I am well aware of the limitations of "common sense" (even the use of $i = \sqrt{-1}$ teaches one that), I see no need for, and little validity in, much of speculative philosophy.

Anthropology and archaeology show us that mankind has gradually evolved along its own path, with increasing differentiation from our nearest neighbours, over the past three million years. The earlier history of our ancestors is merged with that of other life forms over many hundreds of millions of years. At no stage in this development is there currently any prospect of establishing a sudden break at which it is permissible to speak of the arrival of the human species. It is perhaps reasonable to suggest that it is within the last hundred thousand years that our mental development has reached a level which we can agree to call "human". But our present mental ability to think, i.e., to handle mental images and constructs, is the result of the exposure of our ancestors to the many environments of our past history. Human mental abilities, and much else, are restricted by the response of the species, now known as *homo sapiens sapiens*, to its past experience. How can this possibly put us in a position to establish any "ultimate reality"? This imagined "reality" only has some possible meaning in relation to a universe entirely distinct and unknown from the only one of which we humans have evidence. All we can do is to construct models within the scope of our accumulated experience and responses. Such concepts as Plato's ideals or J. J. Thomson's electron, are mental constructs: they have continuing significance only insofar as they match our experience in this world.

Philosophers are not satisfied with this empiricism. In their concern with logic, the use of language, the critical appraisal of theories — scientific and otherwise, — they can hugely clarify the intellectual world. When they pass to the discussion of "the ultimate" they are engaged in what may be interesting mental exercises. To me, vast areas of metaphysics are at best unprofitable, and, at worst, grossly misleading.

One major question providing the background to ontological considerations is that of the status of Time. Human experience of it is dependent upon physiological and, especially, brain processes. In the absence of life, Time could not receive mental recognition. Nevertheless geological, astronomical and other events would continue unpertubed by such lack of mental recognition. Time is an essential and indissoluble dimension of the world as we describe it, where, in Minkowski's objective terms, "events do not so much occur, rather we come across them". Time is an abiding element of normal human experience and it is from that limited base that we are tempted to conclude that in the absence of mind the universe acquires a "meaningless" state. It is, of course, the human mind which creates the "meaning". This is where the Mahayana Buddhists can well claim an opening to start on much strange speculation.*

It is also where much of traditional philosophy starts into various bizarre regions. It is not a surprising, even if quite unwarranted, human assumption that the universe must have a (human) meaning. As this would only seem to be possible if there is a mind to formulate the meaning, it then becomes very helpful to assume that there is some human-type mind co-

---

* These remarks assume the conventional view of time. As space is the medium in which objects exist, time is the medium in which events occur. Time flows equably (Newton:). Einstein modified this commonsense view and, more recently, cosmologists have envisaged an origin of time (as of space) in the "big-bang" generation of our present observable universe. In current terms, this is gauged to have been some eighteen thousand million years ago.

It is unnecessary to pursue this question here. See, *inter alia* volumes published by the International Society for the Study of Time. I cannot resist quoting from one of these, The Study of Time III, Springer-Verlag, 1978, p.28: Twenty-two centuries before Newton's description of mathematical time, the Buddha made a similar assault on the idea of a substantial self. "There is," says the Buddha, "a path to walk on, there is walking being done, but there is no traveller. There are deeds being done, but there is no doer." And then, strikingly he adds, "There is a blowing of the air, but there is no wind that does the blowing." (H. Clark Warren, Buddhism in Translation.) Kant, too, as we shall see, carries his analysis of time up to the level of the non-substantiality of the thinking self. (N. Lawrence, Levels of Language in Discourse about Time.).

existent with the universe so as to maintain its "meaning" even in the absence of humans. Furthermore, that as the supposed "meaning" has been conceived by human minds, the universe has been aimed at the creation of these instruments of its appreciation. By some such means 'purpose' is injected into the cosmic scheme, and with the satisfactory conclusion that a principal aim has been the creation of those very individuals able to expound this thesis.

What would appear to be true is that it is the human mind which has sorted out from the totality of its impressions, those aspects which have gone to form our picture of the universe. The pattern in the universe is one which the human mind has itself formulated. It is no significant discovery to find that the registration of the pattern (and the associated "meaning") disappears in the absence of the organ which created it. And it is obviously an assumption that a pattern or a purpose exists apart from that conceived in the human mind. To the best of our present knowledge, the latter is a very recent and minutely localized element in the universe. In the rest of the cosmos other more sensitive and more subtle structures are almost certain to have developed. Only future exploration, guided by human reason, can lead to an appreciation of much which we can, as yet, not even conceive.

It is clear that speculation of this kind, usually passing far beyond any valid experience available to us, is of little value or consequence. It was actively discouraged by Gotama. Whilst I have expressed this assessment in personal terms, it is, of course, very close to that enunciated by the Tathagata twenty-five hundred years ago. Buddhist students have listed over sixty questions which Gotama refused to consider significant but rather dismissed as irrelevant if not meaningless. Such were the questions of the existence and nature of God; of the soul; the ultimate (or absolute) truth; the finite or infinite nature of the universe. It seems that he was convinced we must accept an agnostic stance on many supposedly "ultimate" questions because that represents the limited status of our human experience. This means we should not delude ourselves with ideas which are essentially mental fictions unrelated to our finite experience.

It will be clear that the Judaeo-Christian-Moslem outlook is in no way limited to experience in this world. Fundamental to the philosophies — and a huge range of them is provided — is the assumption that we humans not only carry with us inborn evidence, appreciation, or knowledge of some "other" world, but that we "belong" to that supra-mundane existence — of which only mental states provide imagined evidence. With this as a back-drop to its thought, it is not surprising that much of the Western world displays an incoherence and uncertainty of direction which is frightening. The twentieth century has seen little, if any, advance in the public acceptance of rational thought.

As a final comment I would quote an American writer (F. M. Colby): "We hide one portion of our intellect from the rest. We profess a principle of faith that makes our scientific teaching ridiculous, and we accept as a matter of course scientific theories that could blow our churches into the air. We call it practical — this intellectual hide-and-seek. As a matter of fact we prefer not to know what our minds are up to."

"What interests me is not that we are constantly doing these things, but that we are so blindly, so complacently unconscious that we are doing it — and that we think the Middle Ages so absurd."

The Relevance of Buddhism

The question should be asked, what is the relevance of Theravada Buddhism in the modern world? Apart from its eminently appealing character, providing for many a largely effective intellectual statement and moral programme, is it likely to have any role in the world's affairs? The answer, as I see it, is doomed to be almost entirely of a subjective nature. There seems to be no way of establishing a necessary positive role for Buddhism. That is, unless one takes the (very) long-term view that the truth will necesarily prevail.

Is that perhaps merely to come down "on the side of the angels" who are, eventually, to take effective control of the human world? No, it is not quite so extreme as that: and for the reason that Buddhism is concerned only with this world and envisages no developments from outside cold reality. One is reminded that the Tathagata's concern was with the individual: he made no attempt to organize or even regularly to intervene in affairs of state. The thesis is (and one can also recall Confucius) that if individuals are enlightened, the evils of the state will fade away.

Gotama's concern was with the individual, his mind and his body; his relation to and behaviour with other individuals; and the well being of all sentient things. He said nothing on how public affairs should be arranged or what structure was to be preferred in the socio-economic field.* He appears to have accepted many aspects of the pattern of the world in which he lived. Doubtless his origin in the warrior caste made it easy for him to accept a hierarchical structure and rule by princes and their officers. He also accepted basic aspects of what we would now call "the capitalist system": i.e., the labourer hiring his work, and the merchant living by trade. Just as he accepted, without in any way approving, the caste system, he accepted the socio-political structure established in his, essentially, peaceful surroundings. The absence of any expression of pronounced revulsion from the established order was almost certainly deliberate: it followed from his pre-occupation with the life of the individual and his aim to embrace the whole human condition, irrespective of the regime which was in operation.

It has been well said that the aim of Buddhism is to raise the quality of life rather than simply the standard of living.

Those who are devoted solely to the individual as a political animal and as an elemental part of the socio-economic structure will feel that this restriction in Gotama's teaching makes it of small consequence. It is, to some degree, a matter of choice: are we concerned with the individual as such, or those aspects of the individual's experience determined by the environment? It is another facet of the age-old alternatives, — nature or nuture? All the evidence shows that both these aspects undoubtedly contribute to the total condition of the individual. It would be preposterous to deny the role of the environment, the historical tradition, or "the economic factor" — whichever version of nurture is preferred — in influencing the character and behaviour of the individual. At least equally

* An extended, historically based contrary appraisal — i.e. that Buddhism carries or implies distinct socio-economic and political patterns — has been persuasively presented by Trevor Ling (The Buddha, Maurice Temple Smith Ltd., London 1973). It is a view which notably enhances the significance of Buddhist teaching.

distorted would be a denial of human concerns which are essentially independent of the environment in which people live. Where life is so threatened by the surroundings that there is no opportunity to consider more than day-to-day problems of survival, then it has scarcely moved beyond the animal stage and then, specifically individual concerns are scarcely relevant.

But the Tathagata was pre-occupied with specifically human concerns. For that reason, his teaching is equally relevant whatever the socio-political system. That is part of its universality. Only a ripe fanaticism could feel itself challenged by Buddhism. The "take it or leave it" element predominates. No-one has ever had Buddhism thrust down his throat. Thanks to this detached character, it is a historic fact that Buddhism has survived in ideologically very hostile climates. It does not express inself in terms which can be interpreted as favourable to any form of state organization nor can it be quoted as being well-disposed to some revolutionary programme, however necessary that may be on other criteria.

Buddhism, then, is a philosophy which claims nothing for itself except enlightenment. Even those who can only accept the Tathagata's teaching with some amending qualifications, can feel confident that what has been "the light of Asia" for twenty-five centuries will become the light of the world for many ages to come.

Accepting that there is no *pre-ordained* role for Buddhism in the modern world, the question of its relevance becomes the more modest one: What are the prospects for a larger appreciation of, or increased commitment to, the teachings of Gotama? Much could be said to favour a positive response to this query and, in some sense, it would be a denial of the validity of the Buddha's message not to insist that advancement will occur.

What is clear is that the teaching of Theravada Buddhism is hugely contrary to the present tide in public and private life. Two world wars in this century have resulted in an enormous and widespread increase in violence: standards of honesty and considerate behaviour seem (almost universally?) in decline: the media, and television in particular, supported by all sorts of video-nasties, play a huge and (to them) profitable role in disseminating behaviour as far removed from the benevolent and beneficent as can at present be imagined.

The backdrop to this uninviting scene has been, of course, the ever expanding preparation for nuclear war by the major world powers. The bizarre fantasy and sense of irresponsibility — overlaid of course, by huge layers of mumbo-jumbo — to be seen at the highest levels of public life, is, not surprisingly, reflected in the attitude of some of the younger generation. It is this flight from reason which produces a climate grossly antagonistic to an outlook so insistently calm and reasonable as that of Theravada Buddhism. The Tathagata was under no illusions on the prospects for the ready acceptance of his teaching and yet he resolutely persisted in his efforts to the enormous gratitude of how many disciples?

If we can assume that the human race will survive, we can certainly look forward to the wider appreciation of his benign, compassionate, and enlightened teaching.

Acknowledgements and Further Reading

In the text brief quotations appear from sources whose authors and publishers are adequately identified. Permission was sought for these usages and grateful appreciation is here expressed for the fact that, in no case was it withheld.

The photographs forming Plates 1 to 4 are taken from The Way of the Buddha, published by the Government of India Ministry of Information, Delhi-8. Grateful thanks are offered for permission to reproduce those items.

Of the very large literature on Buddhism, the following fairly generally available items could have most appeal for a reader not anxious to pursue the subtleties or the irrationalities of mystification.

Bibliography

E. J. Thomas, The Life of the Buddha as legend and history, London, (reprinted) 1971.

E. J. Thomas, The History of Buddhist Thought. London (reprinted) 1971.

W. Rahula, What the Buddha Taught, New York, 1964.

E.A. Burtt, The Teachings of the Compassionate Buddha. New York and London, 1955.

H. Saddhatissa, The Buddha's Way. London, 1971.

M. Carrithers, The Buddha. Oxford and New York, 1983.

H. K. Coomaraswamy, Buddha and the Gospel of Buddhism (revised). New York, 1964.

M. E. Spiro, Buddhism and Society (i.e. in Burma). New York, 1982.

R. F. Gombrich, Precept and Practice (Traditional Buddhism in Sri Lanka). Oxford, 1971.

H. Bechert and R. Gombrich (editors), The World of Buddhism. London, 1984.

This is a large work having the sub-title: Buddhist monks and nuns in Society and Culture. It contains an eight-column bibliography.

INDEX

See Contents for major sections of the text
n = page n; **n** = page n et seq.